I0035923

Aunt Tilly Always Made the Best Lasagna

A Parable About Restaurant Management and Accidental Wealth

James A. McCain, Ph.D.

The Business Doctor

CGW
PUBLISHING

2012

Aunt Tilly Always Made the Best Lasagna

A Parable About Restaurant Management and Accidental Wealth

James A. McCain, Ph.D.

The Business Doctor

First Edition: November 2012

ISBN 978-1-908239-22-0

Published by:

CGW Publishing   www.cgwpublishing.com
B 1502
PO Box 15113   mail@cgwpublishing.com
Birmingham
B2 2NJ
United Kingdom

Contents

Prologue

Aunt Tilly Finds Out It's Not Easy to Run a Restaurant

Rudy, the headwaiter and de-facto general manager, stuck his head in Tilly's office while she was writing a report at her desk. "Marla quit."

Tilly leaned back in her chair, groaned, and cradled her face in her hands.

"I'll handle her spot for tonight," Rudy said, "but I can't keep doing this forever. We're losing a lot of good people."

"How many is that now?"

Rudy counted them out with his fingers. "Well, we had Alice, Janet, and Barb on the waitress side. Not to mention Julio and Rasheed in the kitchen."

"Kitchen help is cheap. We can always replace busboys and dishwashers."

"Tilly, it ain't going to be long before we start losing the cooks."

Tilly sighed. "Let me handle that, Rudy. Look, I'll get Marla replaced."

Rudy shook his head. "Won't make any difference. We don't bring enough customers into the restaurant, the girls get fewer tips. And they live on tips. You know that. The new girl will quit soon enough."

Tilly winced.

"It's all going downhill," Rudy grumbled in a gloomy voice that matched his appearance. The staff called him The Undertaker behind his back because he acted as if storm clouds followed him wherever he went. "We only got twelve covers[1] so far for dinner, and it's eight o'clock. And three of those are comp[2]. The way things are going right now, it's probably a good thing we got employees quitting. Can't afford to pay them with the money we're pulling in."

Tilly got up and walked to the door. She patted Rudy on the shoulder and gently ushered him back into the dining room. "I've got a handle on it, Rudy. It's going to get better."

But she didn't believe it. And she knew her brave words didn't fool Rudy. He had been in

---

1   The term restaurant workers use to mean customers.
2   Free meals given to important customers.

the business for over thirty years and he recognized when a restaurant was going under. As Tilly's junior partner, he had every right to know how bad the financial situation was, but Tilly was hiding it from him, afraid to confront it herself.

She walked to the window overlooking the front of the restaurant and noticed that the large neon sign bordering the road proclaiming Aunt Tilly's Lasagna Factory stood lonely guard over a mostly vacant parking lot.

Tilly glimpsed at her reflection in the large pane of glass and involuntarily winced. Since she started the restaurant she had lost about twenty pounds, and she looked as frail as a ghost with pallor to match. Her face, once relatively unlined for a healthy sixty-two-year--old grandmother, contained wrinkles and strain lines that made her look eighty. No longer could she afford the time for those invigorating and glorious early morning walks. Not as long as the business was falling apart.

She snorted and amended that last thought. She had been unable to schedule any free time since she started the business. The restaurant consumed every last minute of her waking hours. Those fifteen-hour days drained her. Her evening activity consisted of eating a quick meal at the restaurant, riding home in her leased Infiniti sedan (she was dangerously close to missing payments), plopping in front of the TV for about twenty minutes, and then dragging her tired body to bed, where she collapsed until the alarm jangled into her consciousness six hours later. Too darn much, for a 55-year-old woman she thought. Just too darn much.

To compound her misery, Mark, her new boyfriend had been avoiding her. When Tilly called he made up one excuse after another not to see her. Now, of all times, she needed somebody strong to lean on, somebody who could be by her side.

Mark Ragazzo[3] was that person. He had been the first man whom she was attracted to since the death of her husband. A 58-year-old widower, Mark owned and operated his own plumbing supply store in Largetown, not far

---

3   For those of you who don't speak Italian, Ragazzo means boyfriend.

from Aunt Tilly's Lasagna Factory. His absence at this time was crushing her, but she could do nothing about it. She was hurt and bewildered.

Tilly had come a long way in the past five years, since the day Frank, her husband of thirty-five years, collapsed and died from a sudden and unexpected heart attack. After the shock of his death subsided, Tilly fulfilled her lifelong dream of owning a restaurant. She had taken the plunge into entrepreneurial waters by purchasing the small but busy Gilbert's Diner in her home town of Smallville, Indiana when its owner retired; then selling out when the diner became a huge (for a small town) success, and having been bitten severely by that bug called ambition, opening Aunt Tilly's Lasagna Factory in, Largetown, Indiana, a much larger undertaking compared to Gilbert's Diner.

And that's when Tilly found out she had bit off more than she could chew. The dream that sustained her turned into a nightmare. Her sixty-seat restaurant in the swankier part of Largetown, Indiana, close to the state university, had attracted a flurry of business when it opened, but sales dropped off the cliff after the first quarter and produced business not anywhere near the volume Tilly's plans called for to cover her overhead and produce a profit.

From that point on her existence became a scramble to survive. No matter what she tried - advertising in Largetown's Journal and Courier daily newspaper, spreading circulars throughout the university's campuses and dorms, distributing coupons for discounted meals - these and other incentives only ran up Tilly's expenses and produced little in the way of more customers.

As Tilly gazed out the window she wondered where she had gone wrong. Why was her first venture in the restaurant business, Gilbert's Diner, a success, and why had Aunt Tilly's Lasagna Factory (it really hurt her to say this) failed? She desperately sought answers to those questions and more, if for nothing else, than to restore her emotional equanimity.

She smiled wryly. Whom in the world was she kidding? Tilly's biggest concern was her pocketbook. She was drawing money down so fast from her line of credit that the bank would soon step in. And when it did, it meant, if not Chapter Seven liquidation bankruptcy (she shuddered involuntarily at the thought), then Chapter Eleven and the horrors of reorganization and the struggle to survive that brings.

Realization that she was facing the end of her business made her weak in the knees and she had to sit down.

It had all started out so good, she thought. Where did it go wrong?

Chapter One

Aunt Tilly Always Made
the Best Lasagna

Here's what happened: Tilly always made the best lasagna. It was a family dish concocted by her grandmother, handed down to her mother, and brought to perfection by Tilly.

Tilly's family and friends for many miles around knew that her dish scored big at picnics, church socials, family reunions, and pitch-ins. So it was no surprise to anyone one year not long ago when Tilly brought her lasagna to the state fair. It was yet again the huge success of the day, and Tilly was showered with compliments about her lasagna.

No one knew why her lasagna was so successful; family and friends, along with those fortunate enough to partake of this tasty dish, suspected her secret sauce may contain ingredients that may not be strictly legal. Some, of course, meant that comment in jest (but not all), as Aunt Tilly is as honest and aboveboard as they come. Nonetheless, some relatives were prompted to suggest that Tilly should open a restaurant and share her lasagna with everyone in town. Customers, they claimed, would drive miles out of their way just to sample her prize dish.

After all, Tilly had been a widow for a few years now and with her children grown, married, and relocated across the Midwest, it would be a good way for her to spend her days. Besides, her restaurant might be so successful that she would become wealthy beyond her wildest dreams.

So many people bombarded Tilly with the idea of commercializing her lasagna that eventually she began to think they might be onto something. She did have a bit of money set aside and nobody to spend it on or share it with. Which, on the face of it, was a surprise, considering that Tilly was an attractive woman. She stood 5'10" with a stately figure (none of the lasagna for which she confessed a liking, went to her hips). A mantle of blonde hair flowed to her shoulders in waves that undulated when she turned her head. Needless to say, she attracted a lot of attention from the local Smallville male population.

Just about this time, Gilbert's, a local all night diner, announced its closing at the end of the summer. Gilbert was finally retiring to concentrate on improving his fishing skills and share them with his grandsons.

While Tilly couldn't see herself owning an all-night diner, she did see the possibilities of offering a lunch and dinner menu. And Gilbert's drew a pretty good luncheon and dinner crowd. Tilly figured she could draw even more customers by serving her famous lasagna for dinner. For lunch, she could serve cold leftover lasagna at reduced prices. According to all the flattering comments she had received about her lasagna, she imagined it would simply be a matter of time before her reputation became well-known and far spread. She knew that her relatives would visit her restaurant at least once a week, and they would help spread the word.

Tilly needed reassurance that remodeling Gilbert's diner and offering lasagna for lunch and dinner would be successful. She didn't have any relatives in the restaurant business so she would have to rely on the opinions of the successful people she knew.

Gilbert's diner was open 24 hours a day and serviced the long-haul truckers who came by Smallville just one mile off the main truck route. So Gilbert would be one of the best people to ask about her lasagna, or a restaurant that would feature it.

When she approached Gilbert about the idea (who made it a point every chance he had to eat some of Tilly's lasagna), he smiled and circled his forefinger and thumb to approve the idea. That initial encouragement launched Tilly in her quest.

What made this proposition singularly attractive was that despite not being located directly on the interstate, truckers and other drivers drove the extra mile to dine at Gilbert's. To help things along, Gilbert had rented a big sign on the interstate to let drivers know where to exit, along with directions to his diner. Tilly figured she could rent the sign and paint a big plate of lasagna on it with the name of her new restaurant. The sign should be all the advertising and promotion she would need. That, and word-of-mouth, of course.

Tilly thought long and hard about the name for her restaurant. She decided on Aunt Tilly's Lasagna Factory, thinking that like Mrs. Field's Cookies, the name connoted home cooking and a special family recipe. And in this day and age of fast food and pre-cooked meals, people would enjoy, and pay for, home cooking.

~

Tilly wanted other opinions about her proposed venture from people she respected. Tom Cashe, president of the town's bank, was certainly one of the most successful businesspersons in the area. His bank had been in business for over fifty years and Tom knew many of the major players in the county. He was also a lifelong friend who Tilly saw every Sunday in church and at various social and community gatherings around town. Tilly knew she could rely on Tom to give her an honest opinion about her proposed venture in the restaurant business.

Laura Booker, another local friend, ran a bookkeeping service, keeping the books of small local businesses and helping them file their tax returns. If anybody knew how to run a successful small business, it would certainly be Laura. So Tilly set out to talk with both Tom and Laura.

Smallville Savings and Loan was located smack in the middle of town. Anyone driving through the town's main street couldn't help but notice it. Located at a prominent corner which featured the town's only traffic light, the bank had a large octagonal-faced clock framed in filigreed wrought iron that hung over the front door of the building. It was a marvelous clock and rivaled those in larger towns, one that Smallville's residents were justifiably proud of.

Although the bank's façade had been rebuilt in recent years, the inside was reminiscent of banks of yesteryear: a wall fascia constructed of impossible-to-find wormy chestnut that flanked heavy oak furniture, the kind the furniture factories no longer make. As intended, the bank's customers felt both secure and at home when they walked into Smallville Savings and Loan.

In contrast, Tom's office was sleek and modern. Twin computers with large screens flanked the credenza behind his desk, and a moving screen above his credenza flashed stock prices, bank interest rates, and other financial information.

Everything about the bank was welcoming and professional. Its employees exuded charm and friendliness to the bank's customers.

Tom welcomed Tilly with open arms as befitting the president of a local bank dependent on local citizens. He seemed delighted to see her and their preliminary formalities included talk about social and community events scheduled for the coming winter.

Always the negotiator, Tilly gently reminded Tom that his bank held her total life savings on deposit: insurance money from her husband's death (about $200,000); her savings from twenty-five years work at the local furniture plant (another $220,000); and her future Social Security checks, which she planned to live on. Being the gracious and accommodating banker that he was, Tom thanked Tilly for being such a wise and trusting saver.

Then Tilly sprang her idea on him. "Tom, I'm thinking of buying Gilbert's Diner and renovating it into a full-service restaurant. Specialty of the house will be my world-class lasagna. What do you think?"

Tom considered her idea for a moment, and nodded his head in agreement. "Got to admit, Tilly, nobody I know can beat you when it comes to lasagna. As I've said so many times before, it's really very, very good. And, frankly, so is your idea. I'll tell you why. My bank helped Gilbert get going with his diner about 30 years ago and now he owns it free and clear. It would be a pity to see that spot go vacant. I think it would be a great idea to have that location continue serving good food to the fine people of this community."

Tilly, with a twinkle in her eye, admonished Tom. "Don't forget tourists and truckers. We don't want to leave them out."

Tom fingered his vest pocket watch. "We certainly don't."

"Do you think Gilbert would sell it to me?"

"Sure, he's retiring anyway, and I don't know of anybody else who's expressed an interest in buying him out. Your timing is perfect. And, of course, the bank could help out with the financing package. You could put up your house as collateral, and you'd have to provide the bank with a written plan of how you would acquire, open and run, the business."

Tilly thought: A plan? How difficult can it be to serve someone a plate of lasagna? You bake it, cut it into pieces, put it on a plate, and serve it with a smile.

"If that's what it takes," she finally said. "I thought I would ask Laura Booker to help me crunch the numbers."

"That's a good idea. Laura's a sensible, down-to-earth businesswoman." Tom beamed at Tilly. "I see you've really given this idea a lot of thought. Just be assured that the bank stands ready to help you in any way it can."

Tilly reached over and shook Tom's hand. "Wonderful! I was so hoping I could count on your support."

They concluded the meeting and Tilly left the bank, feeling as if she had just won the lottery. If the town's main money man is behind me, she thought, how could I possibly fail? I didn't think it would be this easy. I need to talk with Laura and get her to help me draft a business plan for the bank's approval.

When Tilly dropped in on Laura at her office, just up the street from the bank, it was two old friends catching up on old times. Tilly had known Laura for 20 years, and Laura, a generously proportioned woman, had certainly consumed enough of Tilly's prize lasagna.

One in-coming phone call after another punctuated their conversation. As Tilly well knew (as did everybody who lived in this small community where neighbors chatted freely) Laura's practice was thriving, a testament to her business savvy. In fact, there were so many interruptions from clients it took much of the afternoon for Tilly to tell Laura about her simple plan.

Laura said, "Put all of your thoughts on paper and then let's look at it. Tom will want to know lots of details before he agrees to help finance your business. I don't want to scare you off, but that will require a lot of information."

She recited the items needed to Tilly. "First, the amount of money you are going to put into the business for start-up capital.

"Second, assuming you're going to use your house as collateral, it will have to be appraised.

"Third, what your restaurant overhead will consist of and its dollar amount.

"Fourth, what your gross profit will be on a month-to-month basis projected for the first year.

"Fifth, your projected net profit, and what you plan to pay yourself, if anything.

"Sixth, the number of employees you plan on hiring and what their jobs will be, and how much you intend paying them. That will take a study of wages in the area.

"Seventh, whether your restaurant plans to serve beer, wine, or liquor, and how you'll secure your liquor license.

"Eighth, what dishes you're planning for your menu, besides lasagna, of course.

"Ninth, who your vendors will be.

"Tenth, the number of tables and chairs you plan for your dining room.

"Answering those initial questions will get you started."

Laura raised so many new issues that Tilly's head spun. She had foolishly imagined that all she had to do was bake the lasagna and serve it and ring up the cash register. There were so many other tasks to running a restaurant Tilly hadn't thought of before that it brought on a throbbing headache.

After reviewing the list as Laura talked on the phone to another client, Tilly was faced with a deep, wrenching realization: She didn't know what she didn't know about running a restaurant.

Since owning a restaurant is what Tilly wanted, she began to understand that she needed to devote herself full time to the restaurant to make sure it succeeded. So, undaunted and determined, she began collecting the required information to compose a business plan that both Laura and Tom would approve.

What she didn't realize until later - much later - was how relatively simple that first effort in Smallville had been compared to the effort it took in Largetown, and how much more difficult managing the Largetown restaurant would be, and how it would drain her strength and resolve.

In reflection it was clear that Gilbert's Diner had a built-in clientele, and that predictable flow of income from returning customers covered a lot of operating and financial sins.

Sitting in her office in Largetown, Tilly decided to reach out again for some much needed help. It was now a matter of survival.

Chapter Two

Aunt Tilly Meets the Business Doctor and Learns What She's Doing Wrong: Part One

The tall distinguished man with graying hair said, "Tilly, I'm Jim Phixit, The Business Doctor. I've been looking forward to meeting you."

"Thank you so much for coming on short notice, Mr - "

"Please call me Jim."

"Jim, then. Tom Cashe spoke highly of you. He said that if any consultant could handle my problems, it would be you."

"That's highly flattering of Tom. From what he told me about your situation I believe I can help. As he probably mentioned, I've turned around dozens of restaurants, ranging from fast food to high end dining establishments. But let me focus on restaurants similar to yours to show you that returning to profitability is not only possible, but achievable in almost every case."

"Go ahead." Tilly picked up a pen and took notes while Jim described a few restaurants like Tilly's that had experienced both operating and financial problems, and how his recommendations had substantially improved their results. Tilly was impressed.

Afterward, she gave Jim a tour of Aunt Tilly's Lasagna Factory from the kitchen to the dining area.

After the tour, Jim said, "I'm going to need a few days to really dig into your operations and financial condition before I can make recommendations. Let's see, it's Monday afternoon. Can we meet again Saturday morning before your lunchtime rush and I'll outline what I found?"

"That's a plan," Tilly said.

"I'm also going to review your financial situation with Laura Booker. I understand she still does your financial statements and prepares your tax returns, even though she's located in Smallville and you're in Largetown."

"We're only 40 miles apart."

"We'll talk about that situation later. Fair enough?"

Tilly agreed and The Business Doctor went to work.

~

The following Saturday morning The Business Doctor sat down with Tilly in her office to discuss his findings.

His voice was solemn. He adjusted his glasses and said, "As promised, Tilly, I'm prepared to let you know your restaurant's problem areas. Later we'll discuss corrective actions. Fair enough?"

"You're frightening me, Jim. Is it that bad?"

"Well, it's not good, but I imagine you expected that."

Tilly sagged in her chair.

Jim said, "But I do think I have a solution for you. A viable one. One that can return you to profitability."

Tilly perked up. "Just one? is it that simple?"

"Actually, it's a two phase solution. The main thrust of my recommendations involves a major change I would rather talk about after you understand the problems. We'll hold that discussion for last. The second phase consists of how to address a multitude of solutions to the many correctable problems I found. I don't mean to sound mysterious."

"Well, you are."

Jim chuckled. "Let's start from the beginning, shall we, with the problems I found?"

Tilly took a deep breath. "Fire away."

Jim led Tilly to the front of the restaurant's main dining room window. "We'll start with location, location, location." He smiled. "I'm sure you've heard that expression before."

"Only a thousand times."

"Let's compare your first location in Smallville, Gilbert's former diner, with your restaurant here in Largetown. Your restaurant did pretty well back in Smallville, didn't it?"

Tilly gazed out into the restaurant's front window as if she could see the diner in Smallville and experience the good times again. She smiled. "It was such a nice little operation."

"You're not that much bigger here, Tilly . . . but there's a major difference between the two locations."

"Such as?"

"In Smallville, your specialty product of lasagna appealed to folks who just wanted an appetizing and nourishing meal. Nothing fancy. Just good food sold to plain everyday working folks. Here, in Largetown, you've located your restaurant in an affluent area, where its residents prefer fine dining as opposed to casual dining. Look around you."

Tilly did and saw store names such as Ye Old Tea Shoppe, Paris Fashions, Chocolate Bon Bon, and Gentlemen's Clothier.

"See what I mean? The entire region reeks of affluence. In this milieu the wine list dominates as do waiters spiffed out in dinner clothes serving affluent customers in candlelight. In this milieu the menu does justice to a fine New York City restaurant. Picture it: pâté de foie gras, dishes laced with truffles, the menu in French, and brandy served in snifters. That kind of dining experience. There are a few restaurants in your zip code that provide such fine dining. To be blunt about it, you're not one of them. They're your competition. And, frankly, they're taking business away from you."

"I don't mean to sound defensive but I wasn't aiming specifically at the affluent crowd. I thought I could attract the college crowd because of the nearby university."

"Most students walk to where they eat. You're two miles away. They're not going to walk that far for a meal, particularly when weather conditions are bad. And there's a lot of ice and snow in the winter in Largetown, not to mention hot summer days when it's just too darn hot to walk outside."

Tilly looked sheepish. "I guess I missed that. We do get some college students."

"Chances are they're the students with cars."

"What you're telling me, Jim, is that I'm in the wrong location."

Jim reached over and patted Tilly's arm. "Don't get concerned, not just yet. Let's walk through my findings and then we'll chart a path for improvement. Believe me, it's doable. You've got to have faith."

Tilly chuckled. "Boy, you consultants sure are smooth talkers. Anyway, what's next?"

"Tilly, please recognize that I'm not criticizing you. The problems I'm describing are common to all restaurant operations."

Tilly signaled Jim to continue.

He steered her through the dining room and into the kitchen. "The next major problem I see is that you don't have enough measurements in place to adequately control operating and financial expenses. I went over these with Laura and she agrees."

Tilly looked shocked. "We have financial statements."

Jim nodded. "That you do, but what you have is only the beginning. A profit and loss statement, a balance sheet, and a cash flow statement that's not being used adequately aren't enough."

Tilly started to object until Jim held up his hand to stop her. "I noticed the absence of several measures that if tracked will help you stay on course."

"For example?"

"There are lots of them and we'll get into the most meaningful of them later. But for purposes of illustration, let's examine wage costs as a percentage of total sales. In order to keep wage costs in line you need to track them monthly, and when the percentages start to increase you're in a position to ask why. And answering the right question, such as why, leads to understanding the root causes of the problem. Now you're in a good position to take whatever corrective action is necessary to move wage costs back in line with the budget. It's a very direct process.

"For example, I did a quick calculation that shows you have too many employees relative to your current sales level. If so many of your servers hadn't been quitting, you'd be in worse shape."

Tilly's face clouded over.

"Another example is total sales per customer. To find that number you divide total sales by the number of customers for the same sales period. Calculate that ratio weekly and when you see it start to drop it's a sign of change for the worse, and you have to pin the reason down to prevent it from dropping further. Those are the kind of measurements I'm talking about."

Tilly nodded. "I see what you mean. By tracking and examining those two measurements alone, I'll be able to keep labor costs in line with sales."

"Bingo!. You nailed it." Jim smiled. "I can see you're going to be a fast learner."

"What's next?" Tilly said, leaning forward, eager now to learn more.

Jim flipped a page of his report. "Let's talk cash flow. Something you're not paying enough attention to, and it's getting you in trouble.""

"Tilly's eyebrows rose. "I leave all of that business to Laura. I'm a cook, and a restaurant owner, not an accountant."

Jim sighed and leaned back in his chair. "Tilly, I hate to contradict you, but you need to realize that cash is the lifeblood of your business. Without enough cash on hand to pay your vendors, your employees, and all the other expenses that a restaurant accrues, you're going to go bankrupt."

Tilly's voice turned frosty. "All I need to do is get back on my feet and the cash problem will be taken care of."

Jim sighed again. "I'm afraid that's not true. When I had my sit-down with Laura yesterday, she told me differently. She said that even when you were operating the restaurant in Smallville - the old Gilbert's Diner - you had periods when you had to put off paying the help and your suppliers because you didn't have enough cash on hand. She said that you even lost a condiments vendor because your payments we're constantly late."

Tilly shrugged. "If you have to lose a supplier, that's the one least likely to hurt the business."

Jim leaned forward and patted Tilly's arm as if to emphasize the next point. "Tilly, I can't help you if you erect barriers to the truth. And the truth is that cash is king and ignoring it will sink you." Jim stopped talking and leaned back, silent.

Tilly stared hard at Jim for a moment and expelled her breath. "Sorry, I'm just not myself lately. This whole damn mess has been getting me

down. . . . Look, the credit card companies all tell me that running a restaurant is a credit business. That makes sense because most of our customers pay with credit cards. Meaning it's less of a cash business."

Jim wagged a finger at her. "And that makes it all the more important to have a steady stream of cash. From the time the customer pays with his credit card until the time you collect money from the banks, might take days. In the meantime you're still paying bills."

"Shouldn't Laura be taking care of all that? After all, she's my accountant."

"Look at it this way, Tilly. Laura's in Smallville, you're in Largetown, but even if she was only a

Aunt Tilly Meets the Business Doctor and Learns What She's
Doing Wrong: Part One

block away, you still have the primary responsibility to run your business, and an integral part of that responsibility is making sure you have enough cash on hand to pay your bills. When you run out of cash, you're the one who suffers, not Laura."

"Okay, I get it. You'll help me set up cash flow controls, then?"

Jim nodded. "That I will."

"What's next, Jim?"

"How you're spending your marketing dollars. Mostly advertising and promotions for your restaurant. For example, I noticed that you've been handing out a lot of free lunches and dinners for some time now, with no clear indication that any of those freebies are generating more business."

"Well, sure, it's a necessary part of the restaurant business. You hand out freebies to folks who have influence in the community. That always pays off."

PAGE 47

"I beg to differ. You're not running a casino and hotel where free meals or hotel rooms might translate into thousands of dollars thrown away at the blackjack tables. Most restaurants I know give away precious few free meals, because that rarely induces customers to return. At best, you'll wind up like Artie on the Sorpranos TV show. Remember him? Artie comped the whole Northern New Jersey gang and got nothing in return except the same guys expecting a free meal every time they came back to his restaurant. And they came back every time they could to freeload."

Tilly leaned back and stretched. "Jim, I'm beat. Let's take a break. Want a cup of coffee?"

Jim said he did and they both took a break in the dining room.

~

Tilly told Jim she had to make a phone call and excused herself. She dialed Mark's phone number in his plumbing supply store and a clerk told her that Mark was visiting a local plumbing manufacturer. She rang his cell phone and was both overjoyed and nervous when he picked up.

"Mark?"

Silence, then "Hi, Tilly." She noticed the lack of enthusiasm in his voice.

"Mark, what's wrong?"

"Nothing, nothing at all."

"I can't seem to get hold of you, and you've stopped coming around to the restaurant. There's something's wrong, Mark. What is it?"

Mark's voice showed his impatience. "Look, I'm in the middle of an important meeting. Let's talk about this later."

"Just tell me when. I want to find out what's wrong."

"Nothing's wrong," Mark snapped. "Look, I've got to go." He hung up the phone leaving Tilly distraught and confused, unsure of what had caused this sudden rupture in their relationship.

All in all, Tilly thought, it had been a bad, bad day.

Chapter Three

Aunt Tilly Meets the Business Doctor and Learns What She's Doing Wrong: Part Two

Tilly put on a brave face and returned to Jim in the dining room. After taking their coffee break they walked to the parking lot in front of Tilly's restaurant to continue their review.

""Let's see," Jim said. "Where were we?" He turned the pages of his notebook and found what he was looking for. "Sure, I remember. We were discussing marketing, and what works and what doesn't." He extracted a piece of paper from his notebook and handed it to Tilly. "You've been posting these circulars advertising your restaurant in store windows and bulletin boards. That's been the extent of your marketing program. That and the neon sign outside the restaurant." Jim pointed to the glaring neon sign hovering above the restaurant.

"I think what's happening here is an outcome of your Smallville experience, where tradition and word-of-mouth carried the day.

"But when you came to Largetown you apparently thought the same conditions existed, and they don't. There is no existing tradition because your restaurant is new to Largetown. As far as word-of-mouth goes, it's circulating among the wrong demographic. A food service clearly aimed at college students and working class folks is located on the wrong side of town . . . which gets back to location."

Tilly folded her arms across her chest and frowned. "I recognize that now."

"Look, I understand that everything I'm telling you is unpleasant, but you've got to hear it through. The first step in fixing your problems is to examine what you're doing and recognize the shortfalls. Again, I mean nothing but good for you." Jim reached over and patted Tilly's arm. "Believe me, it's all going to work out."

"It's okay, Jim, I'm a big girl. Sock it to me."

They both laughed.

"Getting back to the point, there are several relatively inexpensive marketing techniques we can apply. We'll discuss those later. For now, know that most restaurants spend in the neighborhood of three to five percent of their income on advertising and promotion."

"I don't have that kind of money right now."

"That will come after we solve some of the problems we've been discussing and get your volume pumped up. When there's a little more cash in the till we can get moving on advertising and promotion."

"What's next?" Tilly was diligently scribbling notes.

Jim led Tilly to the restaurant's kitchen. "Next item on the agenda is food costs. In Smallville you were essentially a one-dish restaurant and you had all the business you could handle. But when you moved to Largetown and expanded your menu from serving your original dish of lasagna and added chicken, pork, and beef dishes, the prices of those more expensive dishes were never factored in to cover their costs. This is another area where profits have eroded. To make matters worse, you always serve a large portion of lasagna, but you can't do the same for your other dishes and come out ahead. Those extra large portions are going directly from your pocketbook right into the waists of your customers. You've forgotten the rule of 30 percent."

"You can't forget something you don't know. What's the rule of 30 percent?"

"It's an old standard in food service operations such as yours. The most your food costs should be is 30 percent of gross receipts. If it exceeds that your bottom line will suffer. Actually, most of the restaurants I work with try to keep their food costs closer to 25 percent. Yours are running . . ." Jim leaned over the serving counter and flicked through a few pages in his notebook until he found what he wanted . . . "let's see, 38 percent. That's way too high."

"I didn't realize they were so high. I guess Laura wasn't keeping an eye on the numbers."

Jim sighed. "You can't blame Laura for that one. It's strictly your responsibility. You're paying her to prepare your financial statements and tax returns. Nothing more. Analytical work is your job. I'll show you later what numbers to check and how and when to check them to keep your food costs in line."

"Looks like I've got my work cut out for me." Tilly sighed. "I'm almost afraid to ask what's next."

Jim took Tilly by the arm and walked to the dining room's large window.

"I don't care where I'm working," Jim said. "I really enjoy looking out the window. There's something about it that relieves stress."

Tilly chuckled. "There's not much to see here. A parking lot and highway, and of course, my sign. I do enjoy looking at that."

Jim turned back to Tilly. "Let's talk about shortages and theft,"

Tilly blanched. "That's not going on, is it?"

Jim was silent for a moment as if gathering his thoughts. "I can't quite pin it down and say definitively, but I can tell you that you don't have proper shortage and theft controls. If I've learned anything in this business - and that includes all retail establishments I've worked with, not just restaurants - if you're not monitoring employees, they're going to steal you blind. It's as simple as that."

"I don't like to believe that about people."

"Look, Tilly, nobody does. The fact is - and it is fact, not supposition - there will always be a few employees who succumb to temptation and steal from their employers. A few, not many. But all it takes is a few to shift your P&L from black to red."

"What kind of . . . shortages do you think I have?"

"Cash register shortfalls are the most common. You still do enough business in cash to make the cash register a tempting target. Compound that by not having daily cash controls, and somebody might be laughing her way to the bank at your expense.

"Another common area of theft involves purchasing kickbacks. Rudy handles purchasing and you don't oversee it. The simple fact is you don't know if there are any under-the-table deals because you aren't checking. And those two items are just the beginning. Let's put it this way: Right now you have no idea how many funny games are being played at your expense, and until you get solid shortage and theft controls in place, you'll never know. I'll show you how when we start our corrective action program."

Tilly moaned. "My head is spinning." She held a hand to her forehead and heaved a sigh.

"Don't let it get to you. There's a way out of this and I'm going to show you how."

"Please do before I faint."

Jim chuckled. He handed Tilly a report that outlined the problem areas with her restaurant they had been discussing. Here are excerpts from that report as he explained them to her:

"Location is probably the single most frequent reason that restaurants fail. You need to examine several factors to determine if your restaurant is in a viable location. These include population density (information is usually available from either the local chamber of commerce or library). But don't get fooled by statistics alone. For example, if your restaurant is smack dab in the middle of a downtown area or near a freeway or close to a shopping mall, it's probably going to draw a different number and quality of customers. You've got to figure out which is best for you.

"Accessibility is another location factor. If, as in your case, Tilly, you're expecting to draw on college students for a lot of business, you can't be two miles away. Yes, some college students have cars, but most walk.

"Your restaurant is near a main thoroughfare and you're depending on motorists for business. Can they find your restaurant without fighting traffic? It almost goes without saying that parking is important, and your parking lot should be able to accommodate a full house and then some. If I'm not mistaken, you have just enough parking spaces to match the number of tables in your restaurant. That doesn't allow for overlap: diners arriving before diners leave. That's not good. You haven't noticed that because you aren't filling your tables."

Tilly winced. "Boy, did I ever screw up."

Jim muttered a few sympathetic words. "Finally, are there many competitors nearby whose menu is similar to your own? If so, you're going to be in a competitive fight that will drain your resources. You have the opposite problem: not enough customers for the dishes you offer."

Tilly rolled her eyes. "Go ahead, hit me. I can take it."

Jim smiled. "The next item is measurements. Do you have the proper financial and operating controls (including cash flow)? If you're not in a position to know you have a problem, how are you going to be able to fix it? Simply stated, you're not. You need to track vital restaurant measurements on a timely basis. This is especially important because of the need to detect trends. Problems rarely happen overnight that produce catastrophic results; they occur gradually, over time. Tracking the numbers allows you to take corrective actions before problems become acute and damage your bottom line."

"You know," Tilly said, "I never looked at the numbers this way before. I always assumed they were used for reporting, not control. Guess I'm learning differently."

Jim said, "As an entrepreneur running a business, you have scarce dollars to spend on advertising and promotion. Meaning that you must get the best bang for the buck those dollars will buy. You need to stay on top of this by carefully evaluating the effect of your marketing expenditures. Too many restaurant managers ignore the need for this analysis. Watch the performance of your advertising and promotions carefully, and if they fail to bring in more business, cut them out quickly before you've wasted a pot full of money."

Tilly shook her head in ascent. "I'm getting the gist of what I have to do. This is most helpful."

"Next category," Jim said, "is food costs. This is a category of costs that can get out of hand without you realizing it. The best way to calculate your margins on food costs is to compare the customer price of a particular dish to the cost of the food that went into that dish. Unfortunately, too many restaurants, including yours, calculate in bulk. In other words they throw all dishes into the same category. The problem with this approach is that when food costs start creeping up for some dishes and not others, you will not know which dishes are profitable, and which dishes aren't."

"My eyes are opening, Jim, My goodness, how they are opening."

"Another potential financial drain is portions. These have gradually increased over the years for many restaurants as the American appetite increases, and that costs big bucks. Portion control is really needed, now more than ever."

Tilly said, "There seems to be an effort underway to educate consumers about portion control. Kind of fits together with what we're trying to do here."

"It does. Next topic is crooked employees. We've discussed this, but please realize there are a hundred ways avaricious employees can steal you right into bankruptcy court. Many restaurant owners are hesitant to accept that their employees do not have the same commitment to the business as they do, and they are reluctant to admit there are those whose sense of personal gain outweighs their loyalty to you and the restaurant. But keep this in mind: For most restaurants, the pay is low (including tips) and the temptations high."

"It's still hard for me to recognize that some of my employees aren't loyal."

"Tilly, the typical problems we have reviewed so far are the tip of the iceberg. Restaurants fail for many other reasons, but the reasons we've identified are the most common for a well-capitalized restaurant. Low startup capital is a major problem, but Aunt Tilly's Lasagna Factory is a going concern, and for the balance of our discussions we'll focus on your situation."

"Fire away, Jim."

Chapter Four

Aunt Tilly Begins the
Journey to Recovery
Part One: Vital
Restaurant
Measurements

Parts of this chapter and the next chapter are based on information described by profitablehospitality.com and various sources of material published by the American Restaurant Association.

Tilly was waiting in front of Mark's plumbing supply store when he drove up in his Mercedes. He spotted Tilly and for one moment she thought he was going to drive away. Instead, He climbed out of the car and tried to walk around her, but she blocked his path.

"Mark, I want you to man up and tell me why you're ignoring me." Tilly's eyes were smoldering.

Mark shifted his gaze to his feet, over her shoulders, everywhere except her eyes. "Look, Tilly, I've got personal problems."

"That's not good enough, Mark. I want the truth."

Mark tried unsuccessfully to sidestep her. "C'mon, Tilly. Let's have this talk some other time."

"No, Mark, now," she snapped. "You've put me off long enough. Now tell me, damn it!"

The strength in her voice made Mark freeze. He had never seen Tilly so angry and insistent. He heaved a great sigh. "It's not you, Tilly," he said in a voice so low she had to strain to hear it. "It's . . . well, I've found somebody else."

Tilly's face contorted with anger and hurt. "And you didn't have the guts to tell me?"

Mark looked away. He mumbled something Tilly didn't get.

She said, "Well, I won't bother you again. But, for the life of me, I don't understand a man who doesn't have the stomach to tell it like it is. At least I found out what kind of man you are." She stormed away, but once in her car and out of his sight, tears sprang to her eyes and she pounded the steering wheel in frustration.

Everything's falling apart, she thought, everything.

~

Back at the restaurant she found The Business Doctor perched on the chair in front of her desk, drinking a cup of coffee and waiting for her. He smiled when she approached.

"Hey, why so gloomy?" Jim rose to welcome her.

"Let's not get into that," Tilly shot back at him, and immediately felt contrite when she saw the smile on his face drop. "Sorry, Jim, nothing to do with you. It's my private life I didn't mean to take it out on you."

Jim nodded his head in sympathy. "That's perfectly understandable. You're going through a rough patch in the business. Never fear, we're going to work our way out of it. Notice I said we and not you?"

Tilly plopped down in her chair; the lines in her face showed her strain. "I appreciate it, Jim. Why don't we start all over, pretend I just walked into the room."

"Good idea, Tilly," Jim said. "Okay, this will be the first session where I show you how we fix the problems. Our initial focus will be on vital restaurant measurements. For this session we're going to walk around your restaurant as I explain them."

Tilly looked puzzled. "I thought we were going to start with your recommendations on location."

"I'm going to hold that for last for a very specific reason."

"And that reason is . . ."

"I don't mean to sound mysterious, but there's a natural progression of your learning curve. Still, you're right: location is the dominant factor. So if you will bear with me for the time being, you'll understand how I'm building to the concluding recommendation which focuses on location."

Tilly shrugged. "I don't understand it, but I'll wait if that's what you suggest. Okay, fire away."

~

Jim and Tilly walked into the kitchen. "All around them cooks and kitchen workers hustled as they prepared meals. The noise level was high enough where Jim had to raise his voice as they talked so Tilly could clearly hear him.

"We talked about the importance of vital restaurant measurements before. We call those VRMs. What I'll describe next are the major VRMs in the kitchen, the heart of your restaurant. There are many others, but I'll save those for your written report and help you implement them."

"Whenever you're ready, Jim."

"Before we start, I want to emphasize one principle that holds true for all VRMs. Use them! I will help you establish measuring periods for each VRM, but you need to follow up and make improvements. Regarding all of the ratios (VRMs), when they start edging in the wrong direction for two periods (daily, weekly, monthly, as the case may be) in a row, investigate, find the reason or reasons, and take whatever corrective actions necessary to bring the ratios back in line with expectations. If you wait for more periods than two to uncover and fix the problems, it's going to be harder to get the numbers back in line, and by then your monthly P&L may report a loss for the month."

Tilly said, "What kind of VRMs are you talking about?"

"I'm getting to that. What follows are representative VRMs that often spell the difference between success and failure for your restaurant. Allow me to describe them in total before you throw any questions at me. Agreed?"

"Agreed," Tilly said.

"First we'll talk kitchen VRMs. Food costs are calculated as a percentage of gross receipts. Do not group all food costs together. Instead, calculate them by dish. For example, your lasagna specialty is one, beef dishes another, pork dishes yet another, and so on including pastries and beverages. Be sure to calculate them on the basis of the quantity of each dish, normally by weight. This might be tedious at first, but after a while you'll be able to accurately estimate what those weights are, and subsequently, your total food costs. Obviously, when food costs increase (they rarely fall by themselves), you have to start your calculation all over again. Use the 30 percent rule as a guideline (cost of food never exceeding 30 percent of gross receipts), and over time, when you get a handle on food costs, drive them down closer to the 25 percent range, but not so far as to damage meal quality."

"I can see now," Tilly said, "that one of the mistakes I've been making is grouping all of my food costs together. But, assuming I split them into different types of meals, how do I relate them to customers?"

"Tilly, to answer your question, you derive food costs per customer by dividing total food costs by the number of meals served. Monthly checks of this VRM should suffice. Just make sure you do check them. It's really a good overall guide as to how well your kitchen is managing the restaurant's food costs. Any unexpected increases in this ratio - in this example, even for one month alone - should be cause for concern. Root out the reasons and take lasting corrective action, Use your restaurateur skills to improve food cost ratios."

Tilly clapped her hands."Finally! That's one thing I do know how to do."

Jim gave her a thumbs up. "Food Inventory is measured as the value of the food you are holding in inventory but not yet served in meals. You should know what your weekly usage is by item (pasta, meat, fish, fowl, and so forth), and from this base, it's a relatively easy calculation. If you're holding more than one week of inventory on hand, it's an indication that sales of the item is slipping, or that your kitchen over-bought the item. Consider either case a cause for concern and get busy finding out why and doing something about it. Otherwise that extra cost goes right to your restaurant's bottom line."

Jim led Tilly into the dining room. They stopped in front of the linen closet.

"Linen costs can surprise you by how fast they add up. Manage this inventory by checking weekly how many tablecloths, uniforms, and napkins you have on hand along with their cleaning bill. Check and approve every cleaning bill to make sure you're not getting ripped off.

Cleaners are notoriously inaccurate (and generally in their favor).

"Are you with me so far, Tilly?"

"I'm hearing you loud and clear."

"Good. The next subject is employee VRMs. Wage costs as measured as a percentage of gross receipts is the base measurement that indicates how well or how poorly you are controlling wage costs. It will tell you at a glance if your costs are in line with sales. Be sure to include benefit costs such as insurance, overtime, vacation, and payroll taxes. These indirect costs often add up to a third of what you're paying out in actual wages."

Jim and Tilly turned their attention to the servers as they scurried from diners' tables to the kitchen serving area and back.

"Labor hours," Jim said, "should be computed separately for kitchen help and dining room help. Compare those hours against gross receipts periodically to keep them in line with sales. For the smaller restaurant, the owner or manager doesn't need a formal report, but the larger the restaurant, the harder it is to control labor costs without a formalized report, and the more important this measurement becomes in the total profit picture."

Tilly heaved a sigh. "Here, as with food costs, I've been grouping dining room and kitchen staff under one umbrella. I can see now where that's a mistake."

"That it is, Tilly, because employee turnover is the quintessential headache of the food service industry, but it doesn't have to be that way. An indication of your ability as a restaurant manager will be how long you hold onto qualified help. At the beginning stages of a restaurant's operation, turnover will be high, but after you've been in business for a year or so, you need to find ways to keep the best of your employees and get rid of the slackers. Inducements help, and yours truly can help you select the best available compensation practices that will help reduce employee turnover."

Tilly said, "How does absenteeism affect the equation?"

"Good question. Absenteeism is an indicator of employee dissatisfaction with your restaurant, their bosses, or the restaurant policies, and of course wages and benefits. You're want to hold onto superior employees, so it's essential that you discover why they are unhappy and do it early in the game before dissatisfaction builds.

"Getting all of this, Tilly?"

"I'm writing as fast as I can."

"My written report will contain everything you've heard and more."

"Writing down what you're telling me is the fastest way I learn, Jim."

"Okay. Then let's move on to the next subject, dining room management VRMs. The number of customers broken down by breakfast[4], lunch, and dinner is a prime VRM and the one most closely monitored. Simply adding up the number of customers can be the most revealing measure of success. It's also easy to make comparisons from one day to the next, one week

---

4 For restaurants that serve breakfasts. This is not true in Aunt Tilly's case.

to the next, and one month to the next, broken down by lunch and dinner. In essence, this is the bottom line measurement for an efficiently run restaurant. In other words, when you keep costs in line you can devote more time to adding new customers and generating repeat sales. If you have other problems such as high labor costs, excess food inventory, poor quality, low productivity, or spoilage, you'll spread yourself too thin to focus on revenue enhancement."

"Jim, I do that routinely, but the numbers haven't been coming out right."

"And they won't be, Tilly, until you understand how to control them. Here's one that's easier and a good place to start: Try total sales per customer. It shows you how much food on average your customers are ordering. You'll find it when you divide gross receipts by the number of customers served. This VRM will vary from lunch to dinner, and should be measured separately, because customers usually eat less at lunch than at dinner, and (although this doesn't apply to you) even less at breakfast, running contrary to the saying Eat breakfast like a king, lunch like a prince, and dinner like a pauper.

"Here's another helpful VRM, Tilly. Seating turnover measures how many customers your restaurant seats in a given time period. A normal restaurant (if there is such a thing - this ratio is really a composite average) turns its seats three times daily. This ratio is a reflection of how efficient your kitchen and dining room staff are. Factors involved in seating turnover include how quickly busboys clear tables, how fast your hostess seats new customers, how efficiently your waiters or waitresses serve customers, and of course how long it takes to cook and otherwise prepare meals."

Tilly nodded her approval. "I can see where that ratio will help me keep track of how efficiently my staff is operating."

"It will. Here's yet another indication of how well you're planning the menu. Basket analysis is a measurement of how many items customers order from the menu. A scrutiny of these numbers (there are software programs that do this automatically in a computerized billing system) will reveal specifically what items on the menu are most popular with customers for lunch and dinner, and which aren't. Perhaps you'll find that lunchtime customers do not buy alcoholic drinks anywhere near what dinner customers do (a not unusual circumstance). As a restaurant manager you might have your dining room staff mention specials on alcoholic beverages during lunchtime service."

"How about customer satisfaction?"

"Good point. You can measure it in many ways, such as monitoring customer complaints through feedback. The trick, however, is to uncover customer dissatisfaction that doesn't normally surface in complaints, but will result in lost repeat business. This can be tricky and hard to pin down, but if repeat business is falling, you had better find out why - what's bugging your customers - then take corrective action or suffer the consequences of falling sales."

Jim stopped and took a deep breath. Now, go ahead and throw your questions at me."

Tilly grinned. "I don't have any basic questions. You've explained the VRMs well. The problem will come when we install those VRMs."

"Leave that to me," Jim said and winked.

Chapter Five

Aunt Tilly Begins the Journey to Recovery

Part Two: Vital Restaurant Measurements Continued

"Tilly, our conversation on vital restaurant measurements didn't end with our previous discussion. You still hanging in there?"

"I'm still dazzled by what I don't know about running a restaurant. It's giving me a splitting headache."

"The best aspirin you can take for that kind of headache is knowledge of how to manage a profitable restaurant and make a lot of money. That's my purpose. The French call it raison d'être. I'm here to help you realize that dream. . . . Shall we continue?"

"Please do," Tilly said. "I'm eager to go."

"Again please hold all your questions until the end of the briefing. Okay?"

Tilly bowed. "Your wish is my command, oh mighty business warrior."

They both laughed.

"We'll start this session right here in your office where you make reports and do most of your administrative work. I'm going to describe financial VRMs. Cash position, according to your projected cash flow statement, is absolutely crucial. Time after time I have seen successful restaurants with plenty of customers get caught short and unable to pay their staffs and vendors even as customers are fighting to get seats in their restaurants. If this happens, you might scratch your head and wonder what in the world is going on. What happened is that you didn't plan your cash needs adequately. So, the number one concern of most restaurants has to be its cash position."

Tilly stopped writing and told Jim, "That's been a recurring headache for me."

"Next, besides your bottom line, is return on investment. It tells you if the money you have invested in the restaurant would have been better off sitting in the bank collecting one percent interest. When you have investors other than yourself, that ratchets up the pressure. Expect your investors to be all over you demanding to know why their investment isn't earning the return you promised them."

Tilly placed her head in her hands. "Laura told me that number for Aunt Tilly's Lasagna Factory is miserable."

"We're going to fix that. For now focus on other bookkeeping entries such as accounts payable. You want to follow it closely, especially if you try to stretch vendor payments beyond reason - a risky business, because the last thing you want is to have your vendors cutting you off. This occurs sometimes when the owner of the restaurant is not the same as the restaurant manager, and the manager is stretching payments to keep cash on hand without letting the owner know."

Tilly asked about budgets.

"Budgets - starting with the restaurant's P&L, balance sheet, and cash flow statement, and extending to the restaurants detailed statement of revenues and costs - are the basic financial instruments that reflect your business savvy. Pay lots of attention to these statements, and accompany them with detailed explanations of variances (either positive or negative), because the last thing you want is an unpredictable

Aunt Tilly Begins the Journey to RecoveryPart Two: Vital
Restaurant Measurements Continued

operation. This means monitoring them no later than monthly."

Tilly put down her pen and rubbed her wrist. "What's next?"

"I hope you're not getting carpel tunnel syndrome."

Tilly grinned. "Don't worry about me. This wrist goes, I've got another."

Jim laughed. "Okay, let's move to the bar for the next part of our talk."

When they arrived, Jim said, "The next topic is bar management VRMs. Sales per customer is the bottom line for bar management. You get this ratio by dividing total bar sales by the number of customers consuming your beverages. Separate alcohol sales from non-alcohol sales. This will give you a clear indication of how effectively your bartender and dining room staff are pushing high profit beverages, especially alcoholic beverages, as well as how appealing your beverage service overall is to customers."

"I've got to admit," Tilly said, "this is an area that baffles me."

"It's not that hard to get a grip on it, but unfortunately it's also an area where you can lose a lot of money if you're not paying attention. Start with beverage gross profit, which is simply the difference between beverage cost and beverage sales. Here, as before, break it down between alcohol and non-alcohol beverages, with wine as a separate category. Make sure your bartender and dining room staff know the high profit beverages and have them sell them as much as possible without intruding on your customers' dining experience.

"Beverage turnover is especially important if you have a bar or wine cellar, but it still applies to all restaurants, since all restaurants serve beverages. One way that restaurant managers have minimized holding too much beverage stock on hand is to persuade suppliers to step up supply trips. Restaurants, for example, that are supplied monthly by beverage suppliers carry a lot more inventory than restaurants supplied weekly, sometimes even daily by their vendors. Of course, vendors are going to want fewer trips because it costs them money to deliver. So you may have to do some horse trading. Suffice it to say, that tying up too many expensive beverages in your stockroom or wine cellar costs a very large pocketful of change, and it's the reason that some restaurants go bankrupt."

"Jim, I'm writing as fast as I can, but I'm having trouble keeping up."

Jim stopped talking for a couple of minutes to give Tilly a chance to catch up. "Bar shortages are always a potential problem, and it's in this area that a lot of shrinkage occurs as employees pilfer drinks and steal bottles of wine and other alcoholic beverages. You need frequent monitoring to prevent this abuse from draining what often can be thin monthly profits. Make frequent comparisons of actual beverages consumed against what the cash register says was consumed. When the actual inventory is lower than it should be, move in quickly to find the culprits and fire them.

Jim stretched. "That's it for bar management."

"Getting tired, Jim? Want to take a break?"

"No, we're getting close to the end of this session. Let's keep going."

"Sounds good."

"Okay, now we'll talk about marketing VRMs.

"The number of customers is the simplest and quickest indicator of how well your restaurant is flourishing. Every restaurant owner and manager keeps an eye on this figure. Many track this measurement daily and by meal (breakfast, lunch, dinner), and some even track it by hour. We discussed this VRM in detail before, but I stress it here once more because of its importance. Don't get distracted; keep your eyes on the ball."

"I'm wide awake and listening with eager anticipation," Tilly said, tongue-in-cheek.

Jim replied with a wink. "Repeat customers is a VRM that tracks your best customers - those who return time and time again. They're a treasure that demands your attention. Nurture them accordingly. Personal recognition by the restaurant owner or manager often plays a big role in keeping these customers happy. That, and of course, their satisfaction with the food and service. These are the kind of customers who normally tip the most, so they are welcomed by the dining room staff. It pays dividends to keep track of what they eat and drink and when and how often they visit your restaurant. Every now and then, it pays to comp them for drinks or desserts, but don't go overboard. Remember what I told you about Artie on the Sopranos."

"Believe me," Tilly said. "I don't want to make that mistake again."

"Bookings (reservations) is an indicator of how well your restaurant is known. Track this number religiously because when sales problems first surface, they surface here. Bookings that are dropping are an early indicator of something going wrong. And that something can be almost anything. This is the time for you to put on your analytical hat and dig into the details to find out why."

"I keep my eye on bookings, and worry like crazy when they drop."

"Marketing costs can be measured in total, or as a percentage of gross receipts, or per customer. Regardless of which method you prefer, it's necessary to know what your advertising and promotion costs are and if they are truly bringing in new business. Track promotions individually.

"Moving on, customer response rates measure how well or how poorly customers respond to customer satisfaction surveys and what their concerns are, or if potential customers in your marketing area recognize your restaurant's name. It also measures the response of people to special promotions."

~

Jim concluded his presentation, turned to Tilly and said, "I've got a serious matter to discuss."

Tilly held her head in her hands and groaned. "Please, not another headache. I've had all I can handle today."

"As much as I dislike being the bearer of bad news, Tilly, this is something you're going to want to address soon."

"You make it sound horrible."

Jim said, "It is horrible. Anything having to do
with employee dishonesty is terrible, and this
has to do with employee dishonesty."

"I'm afraid to hear this."

"I suspect one of your employees has been
colluding with two of your vendors."

"Which employee? Which vendors?" Tilly asked.
Her eyes radiated surprise and alarm.

Jim named the two vendors, both major food
suppliers. "Apparently this has been going on
since you moved Aunt Tilly's Lasagna Factory
from Smallville to Largetown."

"In other words, since I opened here."

Jim nodded. "That's right. Since you opened
your restaurant in Largetown."

Tilly paced the room. "Then it has to be
somebody I hired since I opened in Largetown."

"Tilly, it's Rudy."

Tilly gasped and grabbed hold of a chair to keep from collapsing. Her knees buckled. She took a moment to compose herself. "Are you sure, Jim? Are you sure? We're talking about a man's reputation here, his livelihood. Rudy's been in this business thirty years. For goodness sake, he's a junior partner."

"It won't be the first time a junior partner raided the till to get a bigger share of the pie. I can assure you it's happening. I have enough evidence to hire an investigator if you want."

"I don't have the money for that. It's too expensive."

"A contact in the police department told me a few things that tend to substantiate my suspicions about Rudy. According to my source, he's been fired from three restaurants that the police know of, all for theft, including one charge of colluding. The three restaurant owners involved dropped their charges, afraid of bad publicity."

"I'm in a state of shock. His references were all impeccable."

"Employers are afraid of being sued if they give bad references. Look, Tilly, you have a choice. Either continue absorbing the losses - in my opinion he's bleeding you to death, and not slowly. It's more like a ruptured artery - or you can fire him. That's your right as an employer."

"Or I can just hire an investigator and hope for the best."

"Tilly, an investigation of this sort may take months, and you don't have months before the business collapses. Now's the time to take action. Right now. Today."

Tilly said, "You're absolutely positive about this?" She sounded uncertain.

"I've been in this business for thirty years and I know a crook when I see one. This is a crooked deal, guaranteed."

A heavy silence permeated the room. Neither spoke for a few moments. Finally, Tilly said, "Okay, let's do it."

Chapter Six

Aunt Tilly Learns How to Hire and Retain Top Notch Restaurant Workers

"Men are such rats," Laura said, and giggled. She and Tilly were sitting opposite each other at a table in the dining room of Shady Brook Manor, Smallville's main hotel. They had just reviewed the last quarterly statement for Aunt Tilly's Lasagna Factory and had sat down to dinner when Laura proposed a round or two of martinis. Half an hour later, they had temporarily set aside all thoughts of dinner.

"I'm so glad I never have to depend on one," Laura said.

"On one what?"

Laura giggled. "On a man. They're all rats, one and all."

"Mark was . . . is a rat, that's for sure," Tilly said, slurring her words. "My husband, Frank, God bless his soul, wasn't a rat."

"Exception noted."

"Thank you."

"You can never trust them." Laura was one martini ahead of Tilly and she showed it with every giggle.

"I'll tell you about another rat . . . Rudy," Tilly said, and told Laura about his collusion with her vendors.

Laura twirled the stem of her martini glass and scowled. "Just proves my point. How long has he been stealing from you?"

"Apparently, ever since I opened the restaurant in Largetown."

"He's gone, now?"

"He's gone. Finished. Finis. Adios. Kaput."

Laura giggled again and took a long sip of her martini. "Look, girl, I've been meaning to talk to you about that."

"About what?"

Laura giggled again. "What were we talking about?"

"Rudy and men in general."

"Oh yeah. Well, you hired this consultant, Jim Phixit - "

"Dr. Jim Phixit. Don't forget the doctor." Tilly hiccupped and put her hand over her mouth. "Sorry."

"Tilly, use this guy to help you set up guidelines for hiring the kind of people that won't steal you blind. The damn rat."

"Who, Dr. Phixit?" Tilly asked and hiccupped again.

"No, not him. Rudy." Another giggle.

"You must be able to read the future. That's the next thing on the agenda for tomorrow. . . . Anyway, before I forget, here's a poem for you: One martini, two martini, three martini, floor."

Laura waited for the punch line; then when she realized it had already arrived, broke up in a fit of giggles.

The two women had a great lunch.

~

"Tilly," Jim said, "it's apparent that you've had trouble holding on to good help."

"I've lost some people, but that's a fact of life in the restaurant business, isn't it?"

"Yes and no. Yes, it is a fact of life, and no, it doesn't necessarily have to be that way."

"That's ambiguous. I don't follow you."

"Okay, let's start with a few basic guidelines for hiring the kind of help you both want and need. But first, please tell me where you find job candidates."

Tilly thought about that for a moment. "It really hasn't been that hard. Most just walked through the front door and asked if I needed any help. Or I placed a help wanted sign in the front window of the restaurant."

"Any hires from referrals?"

Tilly shook her head no.

"Any from advertising, posting openings on websites, anything like that?"

Tilly said, "No, not really."

"Do you normally wait until somebody quits before you look for his or her replacement?"

"Sure do. Fact is, I can't afford to take on extra help, until somebody quits. I have a vacancy, then I place the help wanted sign in the window and wait for somebody to apply for the job. Or, I get lucky, and somebody just happens to walk in and apply for work just as somebody else quits."

"Who fills in until you find a new hire?"

"It was either Rudy or me. Now it's just me. Or, I ask the waitresses or cooks to hustle a little more."

Jim opened his notebook. "Okay, I get the picture. The problem is, and I'm sure you realize it, when you ask the waitresses or cooks or any of your other help to absorb a departed employee's workload, something suffers. That something is usually customer service. I talked with Marla, Alice, Janet, and Barb, the last waitresses that quit - "

Tilly's mouth dropped. "How did you find them?"

"From your employee records. All of the women were happy to talk to me. It gave them a chance to vent. And vent they did. One of their major complaints was that you often overloaded them such that they were forced to handle more tables than normal. Every time you did, the customers complained about poor service. You know what happens when customers are unhappy, don't you?"

Tilly shook her head yes. "The dining room staff loses tips."

"Yes, exactly, and since your waitresses rely on tips to make a decent living, when your hiring practices deprived them of that opportunity, they quit."

Tilly started to say something but Jim held up his hand to stop her.

"Look, Tilly, we're getting ahead of ourselves. Our focus right now is on hiring practices. Let's look at what you should be doing. Okay?"

"You're right, Jim." Tilly took out her pen and notebook. "Fire away."

"Right out of the gate you have to accept that your hiring practices can't be confined to walk-ins and signs in your front window. Agreed?"

"Agreed."

"What I have found that works over the years in the restaurant business is to combine a series of hiring practices. Yes, those include walk-ins and window signs, but they also stress referrals from your better employees. On the theory that successful people tend to hang out together - a theory I subscribe to - you're going to find a higher caliber of smarter, committed job candidates through referrals from your best employees."

"That really make sense," Tilly said. "What other hiring approaches do you recommend?"

"There are several others. Advertising on your website is a good place to start. That's not going to cost you anything, and there's advertising opportunities elsewhere, such as posting for help in the local unemployment office, churches, and schools. Job fairs are another place to find attractive job candidates. The point is to use all of the sources mentioned to attract a regular flow of potential employees rather than waiting until somebody quits and you're in dire need of a replacement. Take the time to interview solid candidates from whatever source, and tell them you'll keep their names on file should openings occur."

"Wow!" Tilly said. "Those are absolutely great ideas. Why didn't I think of them?"

"There's no sense in berating yourself, Tilly. What you need to do is start developing a pool of viable job candidates and never be caught short, again. It's as simple as that."

Jim stood and stretched. "Why don't we take a short break right here?"

Tilly rose and said, "Good idea. It will give me a chance to check how things are going in the dining room."

~

When they returned from their break, Jim said, "Let's talk what job candidates are looking for - good ones, mind you, not the type of disinterested slackers you certainly don't want to hire. The needs of good employees are important, because if you can't meet them, you may entice them on board only to have them quit after a month or two, and you're back where you started from."

"You're talking about competitive pay, right?"

"Competitive pay is just the start. You have to provide a job environment for each employee that allows him or her to make a living. For example, making sure that your waitresses have enough customers to earn tips. But there are other considerations."

"Such as?"

"To start with, the type of people you want working for you need stability. The last thing better employees want is to bounce from job to job. It's important for them to know that your restaurant is going to be in business a year from now, five years from now."

Tilly nodded. "Makes sense. I want that same stability."

"The next thing they want is to work in a restaurant they like. That means associating with fellow employees they consider congenial and easy to get along with. Solid, high performing employees do not want to associate with cynics who go around looking for people and things to criticize, and they sure don't want to work with slackers. Remember the old saying, One rotten apple spoils the barrel. That applies here."

"That means screening job candidates carefully, doesn't it?"

Jim said, "Yes it does. And the perfect time to interview future employees is when they're not required. That way you're not predisposing yourself to hire the first person that walks through the door."

Tilly was scribbling furiously.

"The next thing good job candidates look for is career opportunities. If they think your business is expanding or if they have an opportunity to buy in for a small piece of the restaurant, it will attract higher caliber job candidates."

"Is that it?"

"Well, there are other considerations, such as vacation pay, time off, and flexible schedules. But if you satisfy employees on the first items we discussed (adequate pay, stability, work environment, and career opportunities), you have satisfied their basic needs."

Tilly stood and smiled. "What's next, oh great leader?"

Jim laughed. "Next, we're going to examine interview techniques you can use to evaluate job candidates."

Tilly said, "That doesn't sound too hard."

Jim shook his head in amazement. "My dear lady, you've got some learning ahead."

Chapter Seven

Aunt Tilly Becomes Skilled At Interviewing Job Candidates for Her Restaurant

"Think interviewing job candidates is easy, uh?"

"The way you're looking at me, Jim, I imagine I've underestimated the task."

Jim pointed a finger at her. "Bingo!"

Tilly chuckled. "Well, go ahead and tell me again what I don't know about what I don't know."

Jim grinned and said, "I'll do just that. You see, Tilly, interviewing skills are essential if you're going to hire the kind of high performing people you want for your restaurant. If you don't master those skills, you're going to repeat past failures and hire thieves, slackers, and job hoppers.

"Look at it this way. You're in a competitive marketplace. Restaurants, all of them from fast food to exquisite dining, have the same need for talented, dedicated workers. In your market area there are dozens of restaurants. It stands to reason that the managers of the most successful of those restaurants are either doing what you're doing now - learning interviewing skills to select the best qualified people - or they have already mastered the craft."

Tilly shook her head in agreement. "I know what's coming next. There's a limited number of qualified job candidates available."

"You put your finger on it. Sure there are many people willing to work for you, but only a select number of those are the kind of people that will help you succeed. You task is to learn how to tell the difference. That's the purpose of this session."

"I'm eager to learn what to do."

"You can start by becoming a good listener, hearing what the job candidate says, trying to understand what she is about. Does she talk a good game but can't perform well? You've got to dig beneath the surface to find out. A lot of job candidates, for example, will try to seduce you with a smile. Don't allow it to happen to you. Forget the smile and focus on whether or not the job candidate has the relevant experience and is motivated to do a good job.

"Some will try to win you over with a sad story. They're on the street and they need a job, their kids need braces, that kind of thing. Sure, you want to help. The sympathetic impulse is a natural one. But if you allow their stories to sway you, you're the one who will suffer when they quit without warning or steal booze from your bar, or insult a valued customer."

"I've been guilty of that sin," Tilly said. "One of the women who recently quit, Barb, told me that she was in desperate need for money for her autistic son. I bought it, hook, line, and sinker. Come to find out after she left that she doesn't have any children. She's now working down the street for one of my competitors."

"Want to bet she used the same line there to land the job, and that sooner or later she will quit for a nickel more an hour somewhere else? Drifters like Barb alienate customers and damage your bottom line."

"Believe me, Jim, I've learned my lesson. No more Mr. Nice Guy. From here on in, off with the rose colored glasses."

"Good. Glad to hear it. . . . Okay, before you interview the first job candidate, you must prepare for all upcoming interviews. All, not just some. What you'll learn here today you'll be able to use from now on, regardless of how many interviews you conduct."

"I'm all ears."

"The first step on the road to successful interviewing is preparation. The best way to avoid being fooled or tricked in an interview is to learn everything you can about that smiling young lady sitting across the desk from you. That means having read her resume ahead of the face to face interview and trying to ferret out her qualities. Does she, for instance, have a history of job hopping? Is her experience right for you? You don't want to hire Jane whose primary experience has been slinging hamburgers and fries at a fast food restaurant for the past ten years. And you certainly don't want somebody whose careless appearance offends customers. For example, Bob, who chews gum during the interview and slouches in his chair.

"Which brings up a point. If you have a walk in that doesn't have a resume prepared, ask her to prepare one and submit it. You want time to review it so you can ask the right questions during the interview."

"What about busboys and kitchen help? Do they need resumes, too?"

"Most restaurant managers don't require resumes from that level of staff. My answer is if the busboy hasn't been referred by one of your trusted employees, and you know nothing about him, then yes, I would require him at least to complete an application that describes his background."

"What if he's an immigrant and can't read English?"

"Then have somebody who understands his language help him fill out the application. Tilly, if he's a thief and you aren't aware of it, he could copy the key that unlocks the door to the wine cellar and pay a midnight visit with a couple of his friends, and clean you out. So you can't take no for an answer."

"I've never paid much attention to hiring busboys and dishwashers. I left that up to Rudy." Tilly blushed. "You don't have to say it, Jim. Who knows what kind of people Rudy was hiring and what kind of schemes he was working with the help?"

"Yes, exactly. Later on we'll review the 101 ways employees steal from restaurants and that should help you identify potential areas of losses (see Appendix for a complete listing). For now let's move on to asking the right questions during the interview."

"What do you mean by the right questions?"

"Those are questions that allow you to evaluate the job candidate and determine if she is a good fit for your restaurant. For example, you'll want to assess if she's both a hard worker and friendly, because that will predict her success with customers. Of course you also need to know if she's honest and smart enough to handle the job."

Tilly chortled. "C'mon, Jim, smart enough? We're not talking rocket science here."

"Evidently, Tilly, you've been spared dealing with servers who get confused taking orders and communicating them to the kitchen and screwing them up, or cooks who routinely mix the wrong ingredients and can't get the hang of using the right quantities because they can't add and subtract."

Tilly said, "I get your point."

"Regardless of whom you're interviewing, you'll want to prepare these questions ahead of time. I've trained the restaurateurs I've worked with to prepare a list of questions designed to help them make hiring decisions."

"What kind of questions?"

"For example, 'Why do you want to work in a restaurant?' The job candidate's response can be quite revealing. If she gives you a blank stare or stutters around without making a cogent response, she hasn't given it any thought, has she? That's a bad sign, and you'll want to probe to see if she's a drifter. Or if she says 'It's all I can get,' that response should alert you to the possibility that, like Barb, she might flee at the first opportunity to earn a nickel more per hour at a competitive eatery."

Tilly nodded thoughtfully. "Those answers do provide an insight into the job candidates' character and motivation. I can see that."

"Another question might be, 'Why have you been successful in your work?' Here, again, the answer will give you an insight into the work ethic of the applicant. If you get that blank stare again or any confusion in the answer, you probably should question whether the applicant was successful at her previous jobs. Every job applicant should be able to give you a positive response such as, 'My previous employer told me she's never seen anybody hustle so much to keep customers happy.'

"What you're attempting to do, Tilly, is find the right person that not only can do the job, but one that fits into the culture of your organization."

Tilly knitted her brow. "What do you mean by culture?"

"The way that your employees work together and get along with one another. If you hire a sourpuss to work among fellow employees who are dependably cheerful and positive, you'll create discontent among your employees. The cynical, the supercritical, the sarcastic, the negative, the pessimistic, the unenthusiastic character, tends to bring fellow employees down to his level of unhappiness. Hiring the sourpuss is tantamount to inserting a cancer into an otherwise healthy body."

Tilly smiled. "Wow! What a colorful way you have with words. Looks like I'm learning a new skill."

"That you are. Now for one final point. During the interview or immediately after it, take enough time to think about the job candidate and assess her ability to work in your restaurant. Follow your instincts. They have developed over years of experience and they'll help guide your decision. If, for any reason, you have doubts, either follow-up and get enough information to make an informed decision about the job candidate, or do not hire her. Just use good judgment and common sense."

"Is that it, Jim?"

Jim thought about Tilly's question. "Tilly, because you've had problems holding on to employees, I think it's best if we go ahead and show you how the proper orientation procedure for new employees works, specifically what to review with them on their first day of work." "I can't argue with you there, Jim. It's one of my weaknesses."

Jim winked at her. "We can do something about that."

Chapter Eight

Aunt Tilly Learns
How to Acclimate
New Employees

Tilly's cell phone rang while she was driving her rented Dodge pickup truck home late that evening. (The dealer had re-possessed her leased Infiniti.)

"Tilly, it's Laura."

"Laura, I didn't know you worked this late."

"I hope you're saying that tongue-in-cheek, girl" Laura said with a touch of playful sarcasm. "You want to compare hours?"

Tilly chuckled. "What can I do for you?"

"Holding on to your seat?"

"Uh oh! Good or bad news?"

"It's not bad and it could be good."

"Just what I don't need tonight, a puzzle."

"Remember what happened to Gilbert's Diner after you sold it to Italian Kitchen, the national chain?"

"Sure, they ran a whole bunch of ads on TV and in the newspaper for their grand opening.

Attracted a lot of business, from what I was told. Last time I heard they were still doing pretty good."

"Guess again."

"You mean they - "

"You got it. Business started out well for them, then started to dry up. Next thing I know, they're closing shop in Smallville. Part of their latest retrenching campaign."

"As Andy Griffith used to say, 'Well, I'll be hornswaggled.'"

"Tilly, I don't think it was Andy Griffith. Sounds western. Maybe from the old Gene Autry or Roy Rogers cowboy movies."

"Out of business in Smallville, eh?" Tilly couldn't help smiling to herself. Misery does love company.

"Bring any ideas to mind?" Laura asked.

Tilly said, "No . . . wait a minute! You're not thinking of me, are you?"

"As a matter of fact, you're the first person who came to mind as soon as Tom Cashe told me Italian Kitchen is looking for a buyer."

"Laura, right now I'm in an awful mess. You prepare my financials. You can see that. You know I don't have the money or the credit line for that."

"I also know, girl, that when you ran Aunt Tilly's Lasagna Factory in Smallville, it was a success. Problem is, it kind of went to your head, and you tried to cut a fat hog by moving upscale to Largetown."

"Don't tell me. I know. I'm living that mistake every day."

"It's not too late to do something about it."

Tilly exhaled audibly. "That's why I hired Dr. Phixit, Laura. If he can't help me, I'm finished." Her voice trailed off.

~

"The first day," Jim said. "That critical first day. I don't know if you realize it, Tilly, but you can make or break a new employee her first day on the job."

"Do you really think that first day is so important?"

Jim slapped his knee. "Boy, do I ever! Failure to orient new employees is one of the leading causes of employee dissatisfaction. To complicate matters, in today's tight job market, keeping good employees has become almost as challenging as finding good candidates. The job market is jammed full of mediocre job performers. Sorting through them to come up with top grade employees is a chore. Once you filter through the best in the market and hire them, they'll jump ship if they don't think you care about them. Don't forget: Restaurants are always in the market for top performers."

"Care about them? Well, of course I care about them. But isn't getting the job enough?"

"Tilly, put yourself in the shoes of a new employee. You're anxious, probably intimidated, wanting to start off on the right foot, but unsure how to do it. An employer can eliminate all of that uncertainty by giving the new hire an orientation that sends a positive message: we care about you and want you to be successful so we're taking the time to provide you with helpful information to get you started on the right foot.

"Now if you're a new employee thrown into the work environment, in essence told to sink or swim, how loyal will you be to that uncaring boss when another opportunity opens up in another restaurant?"

"You won't be," Tilly said. "I see that now."

"Good. Mission accomplished. Now let's take a look at the type of information a new employee really wants and needs to ease the burden of that first day on the job."

Tilly smiled. "Ready when you are."

"Item number one. You explain your employment policies including pay, work hours, sick leave, vacation, holidays, and who will be her training mentor. You also tell the new employee a little of your background and your purpose in buying a restaurant."

"Excuse me, what's a training mentor?"

"This is probably the one single factor that will either set your new employee off in the right direction or plant the seeds of her discontent and eventual failure. A training mentor is a responsible and capable employee you assign to look over the new recruit, train her, respond to questions and problems, and in general guide her through the initial weeks of her employment until she can stand on her own two feet.

"This somebody must be a trusted member of your restaurant, probably somebody who has been on board for a long time, somebody honest, somebody who is committed to the success of the restaurant, just as you are, Tilly. This particular somebody doesn't have to be a member of management, but he or she has to be a respected employee, somebody the new hire can look to for help and guidance."

Tilly brightened. "That is really a fine idea."

"It is as long as you make absolutely sure the training mentor is 100 percent reliable. I've seen many a new hire, especially an inexperienced hire, get jaundiced viewpoints from a callous or inexperienced training mentor. Believe me, it ruins them. You find yourself in the embarrassing position of having to fire somebody you had faith enough in to hire, and it's because the wrong person trained her."

Tilly shuddered. "Rudy trained Barb and Alice, and they didn't last long. I get the point."

"Item number two. You should have some kind of organizational chart that displays all the people in your restaurant and what they do, as well as where the new hire fits in and who her direct supervisor is.

"Item number three. You need to specifically describe what you expect from the new hire, stressing productivity, quality, and customer service, the three cornerstones of successful employment for every restaurant worker. This discussion takes in lunch and break periods, punctuality reporting to work, what meal allowances the new hire is entitled to, and scheduling changes."

Tilly frowned. "I've never discussed productivity, quality, and customer service standards before. I assumed that just came with the job."

"Yes they do come with the job, but if you allow the new hire to set those standards herself, chances are they will be lower than yours, and you sure don't want that. By clearly enunciating what those high standards are, you're making sure that the new hire knows exactly what you expect from her. That word exactly is important. Both you and the employee understand your relationship (you're the boss. Always make that clear), and she knows what you expect from her in terms of performance."

Tilly said, "I think I've been missing that part of the equation."

Jim grinned and said, "An equation without an equal sign isn't an equation. There's no substitute for stating your requirements loud and clear."

Tilly laughed. "Message received."

"Okay," Jim said. "Item number four. This is a function that's often overlooked, because not enough restaurant owners place enough emphasis on it until they get in trouble. I'm talking about cleanliness; hand washing and uniform spotlessness in particular. You need to enunciate your policies about restaurant hygiene because it is so important. Much of what you're going to explain to the new hire is already a federal or state requirement or contained in a local code or ordinance. Add sanitation to that list and review your standards so the new hire grasps what her role is. And nothing turns off diners more than slovenly restaurant workers: dirty fingernails, dirty uniforms, unkempt appearance."

Tilly said, "That's one function where I spend time with new hires. Cleanliness and sanitation are tops on the list of my requirements."

"Go over the regulations with each new employee, even though some of them may already have restaurant experience. What you don't want to see is a new employee carrying over what may have been sloppy habits from a previous employer."

"I couldn't agree with you more," Tilly said. "I've had to let go some employees because of their dirty fingernails, dirty uniforms, smoking on the job. Smokers are the worst. They reek of cigarette smoke, which doesn't make for a pleasant dining experience."

"Item number five is loss prevention. Make sure the new hire understands portion control and proper control of food and beverage inventory. Of course, this issue is most important for kitchen staff, but all employees need to understand that you will not tolerate theft, and that you will prosecute thieves to the fullest extent of the law.

"Item number seven, the final one, is emergency procedures. Most important is what to do if a customer is injured or starts choking. You should have in place a procedure that addresses that situation. Furthermore, train each the new hire what to do in cases of power failure, fire, storms, and other emergencies.

"That's it, Tilly. Any questions?"

Tilly grinned. "A hundred. Where do I start?"

They both smiled and went out for coffee.

Chapter Nine

Aunt Tilly Learns How Crooked Employees Steal From Restaurants and Bars

Jim said, "There are many ways that employees can damage your profit margins while appearing to be doing good jobs. What I've listed on the report that you see in front of you, Tilly, is a record of schemes I've accumulated describing the most usual ways crooked employees steal from their employers. You can use this as a checklist to heighten awareness of restaurant and bar operations that are vulnerable to shrinkage and outright theft." (See Appendix:101 Ways Crooked Employees Steal From Restaurants And Bars)

Tilly shook her head sadly, "I have to say, I've never given the subject more than cursory attention. Maybe it's because I don't want to think that people are thieves, particularly people who work for me. It goes against my nature."

Jim nodded. "Unfortunately, there's something about the restaurant business that makes thievery attractive. The conventional wisdom says it's because employees who handle cash earn mostly low wages. I'm not at all sure that's true. I suspect it has more to do with poor hiring practices, and we've seen how that damages the restaurant business."

Tilly shook her head slowly. "Whatever the reason, it depresses me."

"Tilly, wherever I find a weakness that exposes your business to theft, I'll develop a procedure or policy that will reduce or eliminate the possibility of loss. I've already uncovered one major vulnerability. You know who I'm talking about."

Tilly nodded. When Jim had made her aware of Rudy's larcenous sideline she confronted her junior partner about colluding with two of her vendors and presented the evidence Jim had found. Rudy started sweating and Tilly's heart sank because she then realized the accusation was true. Tilly persuaded Rudy to resign rather than face criminal charges. She made arrangements to buy out Rudy's share in the restaurant. The entire experience left Tilly trembling and upset.

"In general," Jim said, "you'll find it necessary, although distasteful I'm sure, to keep a wary eye on your employees. Just don't let them know you're watching them.

"Here's a very important point: Listen carefully to what your employees say. Often the decent, honest people who are doing their jobs won't directly tell you someone is stealing from you, but offer indirect comments such as Liquor should be more tightly controlled. Those remarks are indications of problems employees are aware of that you need to address. Listen vigilantly when they express concern about something that should change in your operation. The message may be roundabout, but they could be attempting to let you know there is a problem. If you don't respond to their concerns in a positive way, they may believe you already know about the problem and prefer to overlook it. That sends the wrong message and will encourage even more dishonesty."

Tilly was scribbling notes and didn't look up.

Jim continued, "A great deal of research in retail operations indicate that many employers expect their evening shift workers to steal from them as a reward for working nights. When restaurant managers turn the other way and ignore this practice, the corporate culture becomes tolerant of thieves in its midst rather than focusing on remedial systems to prevent further thefts. Sometimes employers consider those systems too expensive to develop and manage, so they accept employee theft as a cost of doing business. It does not make thievery right, it only rationalizes dishonest acts. The problem is those losses decrease profit margins. If you accept thievery as a cost of doing business you probably will be forced to increase meal prices to cover the losses. This practice is self-defeating because you may take yourself out of the competitive race in a business that operates on thin margins and needs every customer it can get. It's the easy way to get around the problem, not facing it squarely. You, as owner and manager, must make a decision about what strategy is best for your restaurant: reduce, eliminate, or accept shrinkage due to employee theft. All in all, a nasty business."

Jim pointed to the chart on the easel. "What you're looking at here, Tilly, as well as on the following charts, are the 101 ways that employees cheat you out of your hard-earned profits. Study the chart, steel your heart, and tell yourself that you will never allow it to happen to you. Not knowingly, not ever."

~

After Jim's talk about restaurant theft and how Rudy had been taking advantage of her, Tilly was concerned about her vulnerability. She decided to contact the Largetown city police department to get more information of theft by restaurant employees. An understanding desk sergeant put her in touch with the county sheriff's department and the name of a detective who specializes in retail theft. She made the call and arranged for the detective to visit her restaurant.

On the day of the visit, an attractive forty-something woman dressed in a business suit approached Tilly while she was manning the cash register.

"Are you Tilly?"

Tilly looked puzzled.

"We talked on the phone yesterday. I'm Detective Angie Katchum with the sheriff's department."

Tilly smiled. "You sure don't look like a detective. I had a female version of Sam Spade in mind when I talked to you yesterday."

Angie laughed. "That happens to me all the time. Tell you what, why don't we take a walk through your restaurant?"

Tilly arranged for a server to take over the cash register.

"Employee theft," Angie said, "is responsible for about three-quarters of lost restaurant inventory. On average it costs restaurants about four percent in sales. When the average restaurant net is seven percent, you can understand the impact employee theft has on profits."

Tilly whistled. "That's huge."

"Keeps me busy."

"What should I be looking for," Tilly asked.

"Here are the warning signs. We'll start with the cash register. If your cash register is over or under consistently, day in day out, that's a sign that employees are putting cash in the till without ringing it up and probably forgotten the exact amounts of the money they intend to skim."

Tilly turned pale. "I wondered why that was happening. Knowing about it makes me both angry and sad. Angry that I'm being taken advantage of, and sad that people are that greedy."

"Get used to it. It's a fact of life in the retail trade. Believe it or not, I have trouble keeping up with the demand for my services. I can't even put a number on the arrests I make each year."

They walked into the dining area. "Another sign of theft is the sudden increase or decrease in food and bar costs. Assuming you're keeping good records, you can compare marked-up purchased costs against selling prices. If they don't match, chances are somebody's skimming. Here's a good tip for you, Tilly. If they go down suddenly, check who's on vacation or off sick. That employee has been playing you for a sucker, and you probably weren't even aware of it."

Tilly was amazed. "That's ingenious. . . . I don't mean the thief. I mean how to detect her stealing from me."

Angie grinned sardonically. "The tip of the iceberg. Wait until you hear this one. Every now and then try an unannounced check of how much in tips your servers have. Make them count the cash out of their pockets while you're watching. If they're getting 10 to 20 percent, fine. If they're getting 50 percent, not fine. What you have on your hands are servers lowering prices to customers in exchange for larger tips."

"I never would have thought about that," Tilly said. "It's unbelievable . . . and sick."

Angie snorted. "Do you ever have employees or customers telling you that employees are stealing?"

Tilly said, "My consultant let me know I should listen when they tell me things roundabout." "Believe me, he's absolutely right. Make sure you listen to what your honest employees and customers say, because it may indicate you have a not-so-clever thief who isn't smart enough to cover her tracks."

"I'll be watching for that."

"In this business, Tilly, you've got to have eyes in the back of your head. . . . Here's another tip for you, one not based on fact but on feeling. After a while in this business most restaurant owners develop a second sense about thieves. Pay close attention to that feeling. It's probably been triggered by something an employee does that doesn't quite make sense, like volunteering too often for off-shift work when the stealing is easier. Get the picture?"

"I have to confess, Angie. I've had those feelings but never paid attention to them. That stops as of today."

The two women walked through the restaurant while Angie pointed out one possible method of stealing after another. By the time she got through, Tilly had a new perspective on employee theft.

"Angie, you've really opened my eyes. Thank you so much."

"Anytime, Tilly. Call me whenever you have a question."

Chapter Ten

Aunt Tilly Learns How to Run a Professional Kitchen

When Tilly returned home late that evening, she felt a renewed vigor, a sense that with Jim's help, she would work her way out of the restaurant's problems and return to profitability. But it sure was wearing on her. She fervently hoped her ordeal was now mostly behind her.

Mark's Mercedes was sitting in the driveway. She recognized it instantly and was tempted to turn her truck around and head back to the restaurant. But curiosity got the better of her. Besides, she had to admit that her feelings for Mark had run deep, and despite his betrayal, it was difficult to face life without him.

Mark saw her truck pull into the driveway and he got out of his car.

Tilly started toward her front door but Mark blocked her path.

Tilly's voice was as cold as an Alaskan night. "What do you want, Mark?"

"Tilly," he said, his voice faltering. "I've got to talk to you."

"Nothing to talk about. Go back to your new girlfriend."

"I can't, Tilly. She dumped me."

Despite herself, Tilly felt her heart start to race at the news and she inwardly cursed herself for her weakness. "Well, it's too late for us. Just go home, Mark. I'm not interested in you any longer."

"Tilly, please just hear me out." His voice had a whining quality Tilly had never noticed before. It caught her attention.

"Well?"

Mark's lips trembled. "Tilly, I'm dying."

Tilly's mouth dropped open. "What?"

"My doctor, David Rubens, gave me the bad news yesterday. When I told Maria - the lady . . . well, you know, the lady I was with, she couldn't move fast enough to the door to get out."

"Mark, I don't know what to say."

"I'm all alone and scared."

What else could she do? She invited Mark in.

~

Jim said, "Tilly, you look distracted. Everything okay?"

Tilly took a deep breath and composed herself. "I'm fine, Jim. Let's move ahead."

"Fine. Today we're going to talk about what it takes to run a professional kitchen. What I'll do is frame the discussion by asking questions, then answering them myself."

"Am I even needed?"

Jim noticed that Tilly wasn't her usual cheerful self. Obviously, something was bothering her, but he was sensitive enough not to ask what. Instead, he said, "Let's conduct this entire session in your kitchen. I realize it's quite noisy - all productive kitchens are - but I can point out effective kitchen practices in context. You'll receive my report later. . . . Ready?"

Tilly, obviously preoccupied, nodded yes and they walked into the busy kitchen.

"First off, I'm going to be using words like production forecast and inventory and manufacturing. In the restaurant business those terms apply to food and beverages; forecasting them, inventorying them, and selling them. In essence, the kitchen is your manufacturing plant. Okay?"

"Tilly nodded.

"Number one: Does your kitchen have standard recipes? A standard recipe is the base for food service production. Its counterpart in a manufacturing company is a combination of the blueprint and the bill of materials. A standard recipe consists of a list of all the ingredients used in the recipe. There may or may not be specifications included such as Grade A large eggs or USDA Choice T Bone steak. Next is the amount or quantity of that specific ingredient used. For example, two Grade A large eggs or one cup (note that there are two types of cups, a dry measure and a liquid measure and they are not interchangeable). Finally, you have the procedure that describes what the cook does with the ingredients, including production methods and specifications. For example, bake in a 350 degree deck oven for two hours.

"We don't use standards and specifications as such," Tilly said. "We rely on the cooks' knowledge."

"Big mistake, Tilly. No matter how honest your cooks are, they're going to make mistakes and misjudge portions and contents. That will cost you money. I'm sure it already has. In fact, I'll bet on it. Just ask yourself what would happen if you didn't follow your lasagna recipe the same way each time. Without standards and specifications, cooks tend to serve larger portions, and they also generate more waste."

"I'm jotting down notes, Jim."

"Number two: Is the product purchased according to specifications that have been developed from the standard recipe? The standard recipe generally lists specifications for ingredients and they should be consolidated into a purchasing specification or purchasing manual. If the standard recipe does not contain complete specifications, then each recipe must be evaluated for the quality to cost ratio that this recipe should have for the market you are serving. For example, do you need USDA Choice T Bone steaks that are cut only from Black Angus beef or can you use any USDA Choice T Bone? All specifications must be clear. Other examples: A quarter-chicken may be listed in the recipe, but the spec manual should state that all chicken purchased should come from 2- 2¼ lb. birds; steaks should have no more than a ¼ inch fat cap and be of USDA Select or higher grade. This is the format for a standard recipe. Any new recipes should be developed to provide the information described above."

Tilly sighed. "Have to admit. I've been lax in this area."

Jim noticed her lack of enthusiasm but moved on. "Number three: Are purchases ordered after a physical inventory, and according to forecast and specifications? Restaurants use perishable products; therefore it is imperative that a physical inventory be taken prior to placing an order with a vendor. In most cases, inventory should be taken at intervals that do not exceed one week. You should view all in-house materials for quality degradation and either list them as usable and placed on the inventory, or used in another manner even though it may reduce the return on the money invested in the ingredient. You determine the amount of material to be purchased by the production forecast."

"That's another weakness I have," Tilly said. "We only take inventory monthly and don't use anything even remotely resembling a production forecast."

"That's easily correctible, and we will do so. Number four: Are all products received according to procedure? The designated receiving person should inspect all products prior to acceptance. The person receiving the product must be trained to determine the level of quality for each type of product at delivery. Are the vegetables fresh enough? Are the meats being charged by net weight? Do the canned goods match the purchase order (30 to 40 count peach halves, not 10 to 12)? If there is any discrepancy, the product must be refused.

"Number five: Are perishable products stored properly? Product quality and yield (the amount of serviceable product that can be, or is expected to be, produced from each purchased item) are affected by poor handling and improper storage. If a cook leaves out refrigerated or frozen product in the heat for any length of time, the product deteriorates. If lettuce is left out of a cooler, the leaf wilts and browns. Portions of the lettuce head may have to be discarded and yield per case will drop, thus increasing your food costs. All perishable products have this same potential to increase costs if poorly handled."

Tilly rolled her eyes. "Another thing I haven't paid enough attention to. The list is mounting."

"Number six: Are production quantities (meals, including food and beverages) forecasted and continuously updated? The production forecast is derived from the interaction of three informational components; the recipe card, the popularity index (how often customers buy those specific meal components), and the attendance forecast. This production report is made for the entree items on the menu.

"Number seven: Is the production (cooking and handling) process accurately followed? The food industry works with perishable products. It is for this reason that the manufacturing (cooking) process is critical. Cooks are complicated manufacturers because they deal with chemistry, time, and temperature. If a roast is cooked at too high a temperature or for too long, the yield will be dramatically reduced and food costs will rise by 40 percent, 50 percent, or even higher. The procedure portion of the standard recipe must be followed, as must all other areas of the standard recipe, or costs will increase and quality levels will deteriorate."

"I think I've done better here than at controlling the numbers elsewhere, but all by the seat of my pants."

"Considering that you are basing the cooking process on your experience, you've done remarkably well, Tilly. . . . Number eight: Are products held and served according to the standard recipe and safety procedures? As with the production process, holding ambiance is critical (time, temperature, humidity, heat). Serving size and display of product can also have a tremendous impact on cost. Portions that are larger than the recipe portion size specified will cause an increase in food costs. Improper or poorly displayed products will have a negative impact which may well drive customers away."

Tilly nodded. "I agree. Appearance is so important."

"Number nine: Are standard sanitation operation procedures (SSOP's) posted and followed?

The work flow for production of each recipe should be charted and corrective action taken for off-standard conditions."

Tilly said, "Ah! This is one task I'm on top of."

Jim smiled. "Number 10: Are garnishes appropriate for price and appearance? Many restaurants buy garnishes for their entrees. Case in point, crab apples and pineapple rings. These can cost a nickel or a dime each, sometimes even more. When profit is counted by pennies per item, it makes good sense to find less expensive, yet good looking garnishes. Carrot curls over parsley sprigs and red onion give lots of color and cost much less. Be creative.

"Number 11: Are costs recalculated and projected at least weekly? When you realize that inventory must be taken every week in order to accurately order perishable products, then you should develop your basic cost of food (material), labor, and other operating costs weekly. The degree of cost control each restaurateur has diminishes directly with the increasing length of time between inventories. Cost of operations can and should be developed every week. Weekly numbers allow the owners and managers to make management decisions that impact the bottom line the very next day.

"Well, that's it, Tilly."

Tilly closed her notebook and leaned back against a kitchen closet. "I'm exhausted. When do we reconvene?"

"Tomorrow at 8:00am."

Without a word, Tilly left the room leaving Jim puzzled and concerned. Today had been a departure from her normally jovial demeanor.

Chapter Eleven

Aunt Tilly Learns How to Run a Professional Dining Room

Laura looked skeptical. "Tilly, I'm having a hard time believing what you just told me. One day everything's fine with Mark, all lovely-dovey, next day he slaps you in the face with the decision to leave you for another woman. Now he's back on your doorstep begging for forgiveness, claiming he's at death's door."

"It's not like that. He's really sick." Tilly's eyes filled with tears. "He's dying, Laura." Her voice cracked. "It's cancer."

Laura reached across the table and squeezed Tilly's hand. They were sitting in a tea room about a block away from Aunt Tilly's Lasagna Factory.

"It's not that I'm unsympathetic. Tilly, it's just that I'm having a hard time believing his sickness happened so fast. Does Mark look sick?"

Tilly took a second to answer. "Now that you mention it, not that I noticed. But it was late at night and I was tired. And the news was such a shock I probably wasn't paying close attention."

Laura sipped her coffee. "Pardon my cynicism, but this whole thing sounds contrived to me."

Tilly's mouth dropped. She glared at Laura. "Contrived?"

"Has he been sick before that you know of, especially recently?"

"What are you getting at, Laura?"

"Look, Tilly, life-threatening diseases like cancer don't happen like that" - she snapped her fingers. "They build gradually and the doctor and patient are both aware of what's happening. Either that or there's some advance sign, like a lot of coughing or abdominal pains or something."

"Mark went in for his annual physical. That's when the doctor found the cancer."

"But, according to what you told me, he never went in for further tests beyond the initial visit to his primary physician. No lab work, no x-rays, nothing else. Does that make sense?"

For the first time a shadow of doubt crossed Tilly's mind. "I didn't question him."

Laura leaned back in her chair and smirked. "Tell you what, there's an easy way to check. What's the name of his doctor?"

Tilly searched her memory. "Rubens, David Rubens. That's his primary physician."

"That's something else that doesn't hang together, Tilly. Wouldn't his primary physician refer him to a specialist with that serious a diagnosis? I don't know any doctor who would pronounce a death sentence without consultation by another doctor."

"But what does he have to gain by lying?"

"Because his girlfriend dumped him, and he's trying to get back in your good graces. Any port in a storm."

"That's disgusting."

Laura shook her head in agreement. "You bet it is. Now, do you want to find out for sure if Mark is for real?"

Tilly hesitated. After a few moments she nodded her agreement.

Laura found the iPhone in her purse and looked up the phone number of Dr. David Ruben's practice. She dialed the number and turned on the speaker so Tilly could hear the conversation.

"Dr. Ruben's office."

"Good afternoon. This is Mark Ragazzo's secretary. I'm calling to schedule an appointment for him." Laura held up her hand to hush Tilly.

"Just a moment, please. I'll check what days are available."

"Before you do, Mr. Ragazzo wants me to keep a record of his doctor's appointments. Somehow I lost track of when he came to see Dr. Ruben last week. Can you tell me which day it was, please?"

Silence for a few moments and a few mumbled words as the receptionist talked with somebody in the background. She came back on the phone. "I'm glad you called. Dr. Ruben wants to remind Mr. Ragazzo it's time for his annual physical."

"But, wasn't he in last week?"

"No, he hasn't been here since getting his flu shot, let's see . . . six months ago."

"Are you sure?"

"Yes, positive." Dr Ruben's receptionist sounded put out. "I'll check the next available date for - "

Laura disconnected the call. Tilly's face turned white and Laura triumphantly folded her arms across her chest.

~

Jim and Tilly started their next session promptly at 8:00 am. They shared the same hard-working no-nonsense work ethic.

"You look a little peaked this morning, Tilly. You okay?"

Tilly managed a tiny smile. "I'm doing fine. Thanks for asking, Jim."

Jim briskly rubbed his hands together. "Then let's get started. Today's session is about running a dining room. Same procedure as yesterday.

We'll walk though the dining room and I'll point out matters that should concern you most via questions you can later ask yourself."

Tilly motioned for Jim to start and they went into the dining room.

"Number one: Is the labor schedule derived from the customer count forecast? Every night, you should tabulate a menu score. The cashier, a bartender, the manager, or someone else must score or count each entree that shows up as a sale on the register tape or is listed as being served on a server's guest check. You use the count to provide history to forecast the expected customer count for the coming sales period. A standard number of covers is set per server, and the forecast divided by the standard provides the labor need in projected headcount."

"That's one task I do myself."

"But do you write it down?"

Tilly shook her head no.

"The problem by doing it all in your head, Tilly, is there are too many numbers to keep them straight. By writing them in a report you never lose track and you have a historical record for comparisons."

"I can see that now."

"Number two: Are tables charted and stations identified? You'll need a diagram of the table layout. The diagram should be laminated. You use the diagram to assign tables in a station. Depending upon the productivity of the server, each waitress may get two, three, four, or a higher number of tables at her station. Use a grease pencil to draw lines that connect all the tables she handles in a wait station.

"Sure. Makes sense."

"Number three: Are side jobs listed and allocated to stations? These jobs are listed, numbered, and placed in a prominent place for the servers to see. The numbers are then assigned to each section by showing them on the lines that connect the tables in a section. It is the completion of these jobs as well as the common tasks (like crumbing all the chairs in their sections or resetting their assigned tables), that the manager checks on before releasing servers for the end of their shifts.

"This is something I've never really done. I've just tried to keep track of it mentally and make assignments."

"Same comment as before, Tilly. It's too difficult to juggle all of that information in your mind. Not unless you're Einstein. Are you Einstein?" Jim asked, trying not to grin.

Tilly smiled. "I can't even count to ten some nights, I'm so tired."

"Tilly, it's good to see you smiling again. Okay, back to business. Number four: Are servers and other workers sent home when dining room traffic drops? As traffic (the number of customers) drops, the manager should start sending wait staff home. No one should be scheduled exact shift-end times; that should depend on traffic. Schedule servers and other positions as variable, 4 pm to closing, rather than 4 pm to 11:30 pm for example. Meaning the first to leave, the next to leave, and the last to leave. Such managerial control keeps labor costs down and service quality up. Remember to check all side work[5] before releasing the servers.

"Number five: Are minimum cover standards set and maintained? Management must determine how many covers (customers) their standard of service can sustain per server. Use this number to schedule servers. Usually, the number of covers per server is lower at lunch than it is in the evening. A server may be scheduled for every twenty customers expected at lunch but only one server for every twenty-five would be scheduled for the dinner meal. The longer the time that customers spend at a table during the meal period, the fewer the servers required. Each can serve more covers because they have more time per table."

Tilly answered morosely. "Another one of my failings."

Jim said, "Look, let's stop right here and take a break. I think you need it, and you've got to get it out of your head that you're doing everything wrong. You're not. Aunt Tilly's Lasagna Factory

---

5   Work other than serving customers such as cleaning tables.

was a success when it started thanks to your enthusiasm and persistence. And you'll get there, again."

Tilly sighed. "Thanks, Jim. I guess I needed that pep talk."

~

When they reconvened, Jim said, "Number six: Is all possible side work that can be done by servers assigned to them? Job descriptions must be developed that include as many tasks for wait staff to accomplish during their working time as possible. It's not unusual for wait staff to dust, vacuum, wash, wrap, or perform any task that may be recurring or periodic during their shifts or at the end of their shifts before being checked out and released by the manager. Remember, in most states, you can pay a sub-minimum wage to employees who work for tips, even though they may be doing work that is not associated with their wait duties. As long as that work can be accomplished during their downtime, while they are waiting for additional customers, it's legitimate. This additional utilization can dramatically reduce labor costs.

"Number seven: Are employees who work for tips being paid at the allowed sub-minimum rate? It should be common business sense to pay the lowest wage allowable that will provide restaurant owners and managers with the type of labor pool they must have in order to remain competitive and profitable. Yet, many believe they should not take advantage of the sub-minimum wage allowed by many states. Remember that capable and efficient servers have the opportunity to increase their earnings by providing excellent service. Which, of course, raises their tips, helps bring customers back, sells more items (up-selling) and reduces the restaurant's labor costs."

Tilly shook her head side to side. "I guess I've been over-generous when it comes to wages."

"Number eight: Are guest checks (freebies) controlled? Guest checks are just like personal checks; they can be cashed in for food. If checks are not controlled, dollars are irretrievably lost. This applies to all checks and banquet orders as well."

Tilly exhaled noisily. "I know, I know. I'm giving away too many meals. Well, no more Mr. Nice Guy."

"Number nine: Do employees eat during working hours? Most restaurants provide meals for employees that work at least four hours. There really is no standard. Some, although not many, restaurants provide a hand-out meal, others allow employees to eat whatever they want from the menu. A reasonable accommodation might be to allow employees to eat whatever they want from the menu, just like customers, but pay half of the menu price. Some restaurants also allow employees to come to the restaurant on their night off and bring guests, who are also able to eat for half price. This makes good public relations for the restaurant, but it can be overdone. Eating anything an employee wants and not paying for it can cause a substantial food cost to be borne by the owner or customers through higher menu prices."

"Jim, same comment," Tilly said. "Guilty as charged."

"Number 10: Are order pick-ups controlled?

Orders must be accurate and what is ordered must be picked up in a timely manner and money collected and banked. Any breakdown in the process costs the restaurant money. You need a check control system that tracks pick-up orders. Of course, the best way is to have all orders automatically entered into a computerized terminal that automatically alerts the cooking staff as to menu items ordered and by customer name. Pick-ups may also be a part of a food management system requiring payment to be rung up for that item. This is an expensive system, and in most cases a manual systems will suffice.

"Number 11: Is breakage addressed? Any employee that continually breaks china must be reassigned to another position or terminated. Educational programs, such as showing the cost of each item by wiring that item to a peg board and then listing the cost under it, do have impact. You can show that the dollar amount in sales necessary to replace a broken or lost piece of china, figuring a 7 percent profit, would take $100.00 in sales to replace a broken dish that cost $7.00."

Jim stood back and said, "Well, that's it for dining room management and control. Feeling okay? Did you get a lot out of it?"

Tilly rested her hand on Jim's arm. "I did, and thanks to you, my spirits are better."

"Good news, Tilly. Good news."

"Anyway, what comes next, Jim?"

"We move on to bar management."

Chapter Twelve

Aunt Tilly Learns to Run a Professional Bar Operation and Catering Service

"Don't we have two subjects to discuss today?" Tilly asked Jim.

"We do. We'll start out by discussing how to run a professional bar operation, take a break, then discuss how to run a profitable catering service."

Tilly said, "Sounds as if we have a lot on our plate."

"Couldn't agree with you more. Let's get right to it. Same procedure as before. I'll go through the material. You ask questions."

They walked into the bar. Tilly said, "Fire away."

"You seem in better spirits today, Tilly."

"Yes and no."

Jim chose to ignore that comment, afraid that Tilly might dwell on her problems and lose sight of their objective. "Okay, here we go. Running a bar."

Tilly started taking notes.

"Number one: Are all bar products inventoried daily? Unlike food inventories, liquor must be counted at the end of each night. In a weekly inventory, a bottle of liquor could be misplaced or stolen and it's absence might be covered up by sales volume. When sales volume is very high, it's necessary to take inventory by shift. Many owners set an expected cost and profit percentage for bar operations, and then hold the bar manager to that standard rather than try to hold down theft. That's the easy way out, and long term it's unworkable because you may have a thief behind the bar. Remember this always: If any employee is caught stealing, he should be terminated immediately. Should you give him a second chance he'll only become more underhanded and devise yet other ways to steal liquor and cash. Don't allow it to happen. No second chances."

"That one lesson hit home. Rudy's stealing from me has made me super-cautious."

"Just don't let it make you cynical. For every Rudy there are a few dozen honest employees."

Tilly said, "Thank goodness."

"Number two: Do your bartenders follow standard recipes, especially the rule about no free pouring? The standard recipe lists all ingredients needed and details how these ingredients should be put together (and in what amounts), and describes the procedure for mixing the ingredients in order to maintain consistency of taste, consistency of serving customers (including garnishes, portions, and so on), and, of course, consistency of budgeted costs. If you don't have them, you need to set standard recipes for all drinks.

"Number three: Are drinks rung up as they are served? If drinks are not, look for money shortages. This is one of the most common ways for a bartender to steal. Even if theft is not intended, you'll lose money due to forgetfulness."

"Jim, let's stop here. I want to take a break and consolidate my notes. I'm falling behind."

Jim agreed and went to the dining room to pour and drink a cup of coffee while Tilly scribbled away in her notebook.

~

Once back in the bar, Jim said, "Number four: Are all guest checks controlled? Guest checks are just like cash. Number all guest checks and record the numbers assigned on a control sheet to employees. All unused guest checks should be returned and then reissued on a different report."

Tilly's eyes looked glazed. "All of this is new to me. Looks like a lot of money has slipped through my hands in the bar."

"It has, Tilly. But the controls we're discussing will put you back in the game."

"Thankfully."

"Number five: Are banks[6] assigned to individual bartenders? Without assigned individual responsibility, it is not possible to identify which employee is to blame for shortages or overages. This is a perfect way to lose control of the bar and lose cash."

---

6   A bank is a box of money that is used to open up a register from which a party or open bar at a catering event is run.

"I can see that now. Individual accountability is an important principle for both financial and operating results."

"That's it exactly, Tilly. Individual accountability is a bedrock principle of restaurant operations, or any other operations anywhere, for that matter."

Tilly took a deep breath. "Okay, continue, please."

"Number six: Are bar banks audited frequently and randomly? This is best handled by an employee from outside the audited area, usually a manager or the restaurant bookkeeper. The way it works, this outside employee walks into the area to be audited and exchanges a new bank for the money that has been collected thus far, rings out the register, and checks the tape from the register against the closed bank."

Tilly contemplatively tapped her pen against her cheek. "One employee checking the other. An excellent control mechanism."

"It's also a bedrock rule for preventing theft. Number seven: Are cost percentages developed at least weekly? Reaction time to problems is crucial in any business, but especially in a business that uses perishable products. Using weekly operating statistics to make management decisions provides the ownership with a mechanism to control costs.

"That's it for bar operations, Tilly. A well-run professional bar is a great source of profit for any business. A poorly-run bar is a cash drain. Keep that in mind."

~

"Tilly, this is Bob House," Laura said. "He's the agent I've been talking about. Bob has been hired by the Italian Kitchen chain to sell your former restaurant in Smallville."

Bob was tall with swept-back graying hair, neatly cut. He wore a conservative dark blue suit, white shirt, and red tie. Business attire. He reminded Tilly of her late husband, Frank. The thought brought to mind how happy she had been with Frank, and how miserable she had been with Mark.

As soon as Tilly had found out that Mark was lying to her about his imminent death, she unceremoniously dumped him. Told him that if he should ever contact her again, she would call the Largetown Police Department and file a restraining order against him. That ended the relationship for good. But she was still hurting, because like it or not, she had once had strong feelings for Mark.

"Tilly, I'm happy to meet you. Laura's told me so much about Aunt Tilly's Lasagna Factory, and I finally get to meet the lady who started it." He smiled and they shook hands.

Smooth, Tilly was thinking. This guy's a natural salesman. You can't help but like him. She caught his eye and smiled back.

"Why don't we get a table?" Bob said.

Tilly, Laura, and Bob had met in the lobby of Shady Brook Manor, Smallville's main hotel. They entered its restaurant and the manager showed them to their table. When their waiter approached, they ordered from the menu.

Bob looked at Tilly. "The restaurant you bought was Gilbert's Diner, right?"

Tilly nodded. "I bought it when Gilbert retired."

"Then moved to Largetown," Laura added. "Now I'm trying to get her to move back to Smallville."

"How's your Largetown restaurant doing?" Bob asked.

Tilly sighed and told Bob the whole story: how she had over-committed, how she had placed her restaurant in the wrong location, how she had made other mistakes, and how The Business Doctor was helping her get back on her feet.

"Whew! Sounds as if you've had your share of problems," Bob said, and he shook his head in commiseration.

"Bob," Laura said, "I thought Tilly might be interested in moving back and re-opening her restaurant in Smallville."

"I'm not sure yet," Tilly said quickly. "It all depends on what The Business Doctor recommends."

"Think a lot of him, do you?" asked Bob.

"I think the world of him. I'd like to put my decision on hold until he completes his recommendations."

"Don't take too long," Laura said. "Somebody else might buy it, and frankly, Tilly, I think you're going to be better off in Smallville. You did well there before, and you'll do well there again."

"When will you make your decision?" Bob said.

"It won't be long now. How much is Italian Kitchen asking?"

Bob mentioned the price and Tilly whistled. "That's dirt cheap. Even cheaper than what I originally bought it for."

Bob smiled. "It is an attractive price. The parent company for Italian Kitchen wants to unload the property fast. They're not in the real estate business."

"That's why," Laura added, "you had best decide quickly. This property is not going to last long."

"Stop selling, Laura," Tilly said and grinned.

Bob smiled. "You sound like my former wife, Tilly. Direct, and to the point."

"Divorced?" Tilly said.

Bob frowned. "No, widowed."

"Me, too."

"I know. Laura told me."

They both looked at Laura and laughed. Laura blushed.

"Did Italian Kitchen rebuild the restaurant?" Tilly asked Bob.

"That's another attractive feature," Laura said. "They decided to keep the original charm of the place and just refreshed the building. In essence, it's just as you sold it."

"Tell you what, Tilly," Bob said. "Why don't we discuss this over dinner?"

Their eyes met, and for a moment, Tilly thought she detected a gleam in Bob's eye. "Why, I'd like that, Bob." She had to admit he was an attractive man.

They set the date and as they were leaving the restaurant, Laura leaned over and whispered, "You go, girl. I saw the way you looked at Bob."

Tilly dismissed Laura's comment, but she had to admit she was looking forward to seeing Bob, again. And not just for discussing the Smallville restaurant property.

~

Jim and Tilly were in the kitchen. "Next up, Tilly, is catering services. You can manage this function and make it profitable by following the guidelines listed as follows:

"Number one: Are meals and beverages inventoried pre- and post-event? Take care to assure that you charge all items related to an event and not to regular bar and restaurant operations. And usage of consumable goods can only be determined by an accurate inventory before and after the event."

"Unfortunately, that's something we have never done. We throw all catering costs into the pot."

"From now on, that's a no no, Tilly. . . . Number two: Are separate banks available and used? Accountability for money depends on separate banks. Commingling of funds with regular restaurant and bar operations opens the door to errors and potential larceny.

"Number three: Are separate production sheets used for each event? This is the only way to align the food expense for an event with the money produced at that event. Here again, commingling of any of the costs associated with events will hide the true profit or loss.

"Number four: Is each event costed and evaluated for profit? The end result of tracking costs and sales is to determine whether or not the event was profitable. Use that information for planning future events. You can also base bonuses and incentives for the event so that they don't have a negative impact on the restaurant and bar profit and loss statement."

Tilly said, "I can see now where total isolation of financial results makes a great deal of sense."

"Number five: Are all equipment, linen, utensils, and sundry supplies controlled? These items are expensive and easily disappear. Both employees and customers walk out with pocketable items frequently unless you have the right controls in place. Pre and post-inventory check of all items are necessary, both going out and coming back.

"Number six: Are separate time cards used for each catering event? Labor must be correctly charged to each event. Accurate compilation of every cost associated with each event will provide the information necessary to bid or price and accept or refuse future events.

"That's it, Tilly. Short and to the point."

"Jim, I'm looking forward to discussing location."

"That's the last item on my list, and probably the most important. I'm saving it for last."

"It can't come soon enough. I want to tell you of a meeting I had with Bob House, the agent selling my former property in Smallville."

Chapter Thirteen

Aunt Tilly Learns
What Marketing
Techniques Work
Best in the
Restaurant Business

Jim briskly rubbed his hands together. "Let's talk marketing, one of my favorite subjects."

"I'm ready, oh great leader, pen and notebook in hand."

Jim beamed. "Hey, it's great to see that your spirits have picked up."

Tilly returned the smile. "They have, thanks to you." She hadn't yet told him about meeting Bob House, nor the availability of her former restaurant in Smallville. Both thoughts excited her.

"We'll take advantage of your high and discuss some marketing and promotional techniques I have seen work over the years. No theory, just plain hard facts.

"We'll start with general recommendations, then get specific. First on the list, get good press."

Tilly put a pen to her mouth and thought about it. "How do I do that? Just call the newspapers and TV stations and ask for somebody to review our menu?"

"That's not a bad idea, but probably the better way is to host events, say for the American Heart Association or American Cancer Society. That will attract the media. Another idea is to contribute perishable food to charities. For example, donut shops give away donuts they don't sell within a day or two."

Tilly snapped her fingers. "I've got another great idea. I can write articles on food preparation for the local newspaper. That's sure to get good press."

"That's the way to think. And if you're creative you don't have to spend a ton of money on advertising.

"You can take advantage of your lasagna specialty by inviting a food critic, or what passes for one on TV and in the newspaper, to sample your lasagna. That should also result in free publicity. Everybody loves a free meal."

"Now why in the world didn't I think of that?" Tilly said. "Particularly since I did that once when I ran the restaurant in Smallville, and it resulted in increased sales. I must be getting old."

"I'll ignore that last comment. . . . The next suggestion is to create a blog for Aunt Tilly's Lasagna Factory. Nowadays, all younger people - for example, your college crowd - and many if not most adults have access to the Internet and use it, and they love to read new information. In your case, take a look at your menu, and specials and advertise them in cyberspace. Specials, in particular, attract a lot of attention by potential diners shopping around to see where their family will eat lunch or dinner."

Tilly grimaced. "I imagine I'm losing my share of the younger adult business."

Jim said, "That you are. You're also losing business by not advertising on Facebook and Twitter. Millions of people read entries and tweets. It's also a good place to advertise your specials. You have a vast audience." Jim stopped for a moment and thought. "You know, this would be a good place to advertise take-out orders."

"I guess I haven't been giving that part of my business a lot of attention. I can see where blogging has its advantages."

"The nice part about it is that it's free. Go online and go to WordPress or Google's Blogger.com or a dozen of other free blogs and develop your own blog. Or pay a college kid $50 and he'll develop a blog for you in a jiffy."

"You know, Jim, your comment sparked an idea. YouTube is the rage. What do you think of me engaging a knowledgeable college kid to develop a short video clip for YouTube, showing me baking my lasagna specialty?"

Jim gave Tilly a thumbs up. "Now that's the type of thinking that's going to produce sales."

Tilly beamed.

"Tilly, let me ask you a question. What's your best merchandising tool?"

Tilly leaned back in her chair and puffed her cheeks while she considered Jim's question. "I don't know, maybe our menu?"

"You put your finger on it, because that's where you display your product. So maybe a menu redesign is in order. You can also send the new menu to your customer list and places like the TV and radio stations."

"Wow, there appears to be a lot of marketing potential I'm overlooking."

"Another web related technique is email marketing. It's much, much cheaper than direct mail marketing, more timely, and you can reach a large targeted audience. Using college students as an example, you can email them your specials and take-out orders."

"I'm almost afraid to ask what's next. You have so many new ideas I can't write them down fast enough."

Jim laughed. "Thanks for the compliment. We are sparking a lot of ideas here - this is an effective two-person brainstorming session. We'll eliminate the confusion by writing down a marketing program with timetables and persons in your restaurant assigned to handle each and every marketing idea."

"Jim. as I'm sitting here I'm also thinking about how to effectively use a blog. How about a

Chef's Tips for the Kitchen? Sort of a Rachael Ray online."

"That is a good idea. You can also include a wine list and beer additions. Both attract people who savor fine drinking."

Tilly said, "We could also have a featured recipes section of the blog. My goodness, there are so many ideas."

"We'll cull out the least attractive ideas and prioritize the rest."

Tilly shook her head in amazement. "We're really cooking now . . . if you'll excuse the pun."

"Here's another thought, Tilly. February is winding down and March is almost on us. Let me read you a promotional circular a restaurant owner and I wrote.

"'Why not encourage your customers to shake off the winter doldrums and spring into spring by offering the following promotions this March?

"'Festival fun. Invite your customers to celebrate the festive carnival season at your restaurant.

Carnival refers to the days of foolishness and revelry preceding the start of Lent on Ash Wednesday. Popular carnivals take place throughout Spain and in Venice, Italy. Throw a European carnival, complete with celebratory food and the colors and sights of a street fair. Offer flavorful Venetian dishes such as a Polenta Pie, with veal and vegetables, or traditional Spanish dishes such as paella.' Tilly, you don't have to stick to lasagna and American dishes."

"I've been thinking of extending my menu to international favorites. This might be a good way to do it."

"'Have your servers don bright-color masks. Hire a juggler to travel from table to table to create the merry mood of a street festival, and hang flags from the country or countries you choose to focus on'"

"That might be a little too much for me."

"It might catch on with the younger crowd."

"True."

"'Hold an ides of March party on Friday, March 15. In the ancient Roman calendar, the days of the month were not numbered, but divided into three sections. The ides, one of the three divisions, fell on the 15th day of March. Julius Caesar was assassinated on the ides of March in 44 B.C. To recognize the day, have a chef toss tableside Caesar salads. Serve other traditional Roman dishes such as the rich spaghetti alla carbonara, with bacon and Parmesan and pecorino cheeses. Distribute garlands for servers to wear on their heads, and have your host dress in a toga.'"

"My, my," Tilly said. "You are full of ideas. I didn't know you tended to the artistic side."

Jim kept reading, "'Bring a little luck of the Irish to your customers on St. Patrick's Day, by holding a contest. Put a jar of green jelly beans at the front of the restaurant and award a certificate for a free dinner-for-two to the customer who comes closest to guessing the number of beans in the jar. Be sure to leave a place on the entry form for the customer's name and address. Use the entry forms to add to your mailing list, including his or her email address.

"'You can also mark spring's arrival by offering a special menu featuring seasonal dishes such as pasta primavera, a baby-vegetable medley or fresh asparagus with hollandaise sauce. Conduct a coloring contest for children; invite them to draw a picture depicting their favorite spring activity. See if a neighborhood toy store will team up on the promotion and donate a gift certificate for the winner. Display the spring pictures at the front of the restaurant, creating a colorful collage of original art.'"

"You've given me a lot to think about, Jim, and I thank you for it."

"The bottom line, Tilly, is that if you use your imagination, you have many sources of marketing and promotional ideas available to you."

Chapter Fourteen

Aunt Tilly Learns How to Run Office and Administrative Operations for a Restaurant

As promised, Bob House took Tilly to dinner. They ate at an upscale seafood restaurant on the Wabash River in Largetown. Over cocktails they watched as patterns of light and shadow dappled the river's current.

"Laura called me today," Bob said.

Tilly sipped her martini. "She's been all over me to return to Smallville. I don't know if I want to. More to the point, I'm not really sure it's the best thing for me."

"Why not?" Bob said. "From what I've heard, your restaurant was quite successful there. It seems like a natural move."

"It's not that. When I left Smallville it was because I wanted to start a new phase in my life. Smallville is where Frank and I lived, and . . ." Her voice trailed off and her eyes became distant.

Bob reached across the table and held her hand. "I understand, Tilly. I had the same reaction when my Linda passed away. That's when I moved from Middleburg, where we spent our entire lives, to Smallville. But you know something, Tilly, I found out you can't run away from your feelings, no matter where you are."

Bob squeezed Tilly's hand and their eyes met. "I want you to promise me one thing."

Tilly remained silent but held his gaze.

"That you'll follow The Business Doctor's recommendation. I've never met him, but what I've heard from both Laura and you, he has a genuine respect for his clients and his recommendations work wonders. As far as your personal feelings about returning to Smallville, I promise to help you make the adjustment."

"You'll do that for me, Bob?"

"Yes, and I mean that sincerely."

Tilly smiled. "You know, I think this is going to be the start of a beautiful friendship."

~

Jim and Tilly resumed the formal part of their discussions. "The subject, today," Jim said, "is restaurant office and administrative functions. I realize it's nowhere near as interesting as dining room, kitchen, and bar operations, but it's critical for any restaurant manager to understand. Many restaurant failures are due to sloppy administrative procedures."

Tilly said she understood. "I have to admit, it's probably my weakest area. I love the cooking part of restaurant work, and talking to customers, but not the paperwork or administrative side of the business."

"My purpose," Jim said, "is to help you simplify those procedures wherever possible. . . . As before, I'll address the subjects through questions. Ready?"

Tilly said she was.

"Okay" Jim said. Here's number one: Are all required forms from inspections completed and posted? There are O.S.H.A. forms as well as various health inspection forms that the law obliges you to have. In most states, health inspections and ratings are required to be posted in public view. And don't forget licenses and permits."

"We follow legal requirements routinely. We're pretty much up on food preparation laws."

"Okay, sounds good. . . . Number two: Are all banks randomly pulled and audited? Check who is doing the pulling. Ask yourself if collusion can occur. Random pulling is critical, as is the frequency; it must occur at least three times a week for each regular bank, and don't forget to include weekends on a regular basis if you're open.

"Number three: Are all employee files correct and up-to-date, including I-9s?[7] The restaurant industry is notorious for hiring many people without checking their right to legally work in the United States. A well known chain serving Mexican-American-Creole style foods that started in the South was fined over one million dollars for hiring illegal aliens."

"I don't hire illegals, Jim."

7A document verifying that an employee is a citizen of the USA or holds legal immigration papers.

"Not that you know of, Tilly."

"What's that supposed to mean?"

"You don't check their I-9s."

Tilly met Jim's gaze. "No, I guess I don't. Well, that's something else to attend to."

"Number four: Is payroll documented, including cash payments? The restaurant industry is infamous for paying under the table. This means that restaurants sometimes pay workers in cash, without withholding taxes. If you're leaning this way, I suggest that you discuss pay practices with your legal counsel before you get in trouble with the immigration service."

Tilly reassured Jim that her restaurant follows legal requirements to the letter.

"Payment may also be in food. This will certainly increase food costs, although you'll partially recoup because of lower labor costs.

"Number five: Are petty cash slips used and audited? The owner must sign for any cash taken from the till. Accountability for every dollar is critical in a cash business. If the owner takes money without signing for it, employees may feel they are also entitled."

Tilly shook her head. "I have to confess, I've been guilty of that sin. But no more."

"Number six: Is a physical inventory taken by your accountant at least quarterly? This is not to be confused with the weekly inventory whose purpose is to place orders for vendors' products. The inventory I'm talking about is taken by someone other than the restaurant manager. Juggling the inventory to decrease food costs happens quite often as does selling food out the back door. Catering functions that the owner doesn't know about, or that the manager is personally supervising and not declaring as income, occur with some degree of regularity and can be unearthed by inventories conducted by impartial third parties, like your accountant. A lot of money can be lost unless controls are in place. Need I remind you of Rudy?"

"Tilly nodded. "Enough said."

"Number seven: Are deposits made at least daily? Accumulated cash and checks are an invitation to crime. Most municipal police departments are happy to provide an escort to restaurant workers when they're taking money from the restaurant to the bank. Cash and checks should not be held overnight; instead, make deposits every working day."

Tilly told Jim about her restaurant theft review with Angie Katchum. "She volunteered to have police officers escort us when we take cash to the bank. I'm taking her up on it."

"Good idea, Tilly. Another hole plugged up. Number eight: Are discounts taken for quick payments to vendors? Many restaurants do not take advantage of discounts even though vendors offer them. If a vendor does not offer discounts, ask for them.

"Number nine: Are vendors that do not offer discounts paid monthly? If you are not able to get discounts for payments within ten days, try to get a monthly account payment schedule.

"Number 10: Are all payments to vendors made from receiving invoices and not from monthly statements? Paying via a monthly statement is not a good practice. Changes to product received, like a backorder or refused shipment, often show up on a statement. Double payments can occur. Even when you find mistakes and get the money credited to your restaurant by a vendor, the vendor has had the use of your scarce cash resources.

"Number 11: Are all contracts and receiving documents reconciled to assure correct prices are being charged and paid at least weekly? Weekly reconciliation is a must. Not only do you want to pay the correct prices and catch errors quickly, but weekly reconciliation is necessary in order to run an accurate weekly trial balance."

Tilly said, "We do that. Laura showed us how."

"Number 12: Are incoming data and reports accurately reported in a timely manner (weekly and monthly)? Certainly a weekly operating report is better than a monthly operating report. Reaction to problems can occur four times faster than it can when a monthly report is obtained; but a monthly operating report is better than a quarterly operating report, and so on. Remember, money can disappear through product loss in a restaurant and never found. Such losses will be diffused in a month's worth of volume and never recovered. The principle is to drill down reporting to the lowest level of control necessary to detect variances and correct problems before they damage cash flow or profitability.

"Number 13: Are all products from vendors purchased through bidding, which includes at least three bidders, and are bids renewed at least annually?

The good old boy system of quid pro quo is used in many restaurants, with the restaurant owners coming out on the bottom. Keep both vendors and your buyers honest by opening bids with some type of ceremony at which all bidders are present."

"That's a weakness, Jim, as you know."

"We're going to install a system to handle bidding, Tilly. So don't be concerned."

"I know, Jim, and I'm grateful."

"Well, that's it, Tilly."

"I've learned so much this week. I have to wonder how I've managed to survive in this business for so long."

"Honestly, it was catching up with you. You were close to going under."

Tilly shuddered.

"In any respect, all of that is about to change."

Chapter Fifteen

Aunt Tilly Discovers the Most Common Reasons for Restaurant Failures and How to Prevent Them

"Tilly, you're going to find this next topic both interesting and instructive. What we're going to discuss is the more common reasons restaurants fail and how to prevent them."

"Sort of like the first two sessions we had together, right, Jim?"[8]

"Actually, those first two sessions focused exclusively on Aunt Tilly's Lasagna Factory. This session is descriptive of restaurants in general, from fast food places and diners to upscale restaurants, and in locations from rural to suburban to urban."

"Do any of those failures or recommendations have anything to do with me?"

"They spill over, regardless of what kind of restaurant you manage. The value of studying restaurant failures and corrective actions is so you don't make the same mistakes."

Tilly nodded. "Okay, chief, I'm with you. Fire away."

8　See chapters two and three.

"That I will. We'll start here. You could set yourself up for failure without realizing it, if you are not keeping up with spying and researching current restaurant trends, and knowing how your competition is profiting from them."

Tilly jumped in. "Whoa! Hold, on, Jim. Spying? Isn't that unethical?"

"Not in the least. In this sense it means discovering what your competitions' lunch and dinner prices are, the promotions they run, whether their restaurants are filled, the demographics of their patrons, the ambiance of their dining rooms, and how courteous their server staff is. Those basic kinds of things that spell the difference between success and failure in the restaurant business. Perhaps if I had used the word investigating rather than spying, it wouldn't have got your dander up."

Tilly chuckled. "Okay, point taken. Proceed."

"You can best investigate what your competition is doing and how well they are doing by eating at their restaurants. And while you're at it, keep your eyes and ears open to trends. For example, if someone were to ask you what the top three hottest restaurant trends are, could you answer? If not, start right now or your competitors could beat you to the punch and start taking customers away from you."

"Makes sense. Staying current with market trends is important."

Jim said, "Becoming more flexible, adapting and not resisting restaurant trends and industry changes, will put you in a better position to succeed, increase future profits, and reduce the chances of becoming another restaurant failure statistic."

"Sure, that follows," Tilly said in agreement.

"Along that same line of thought, if you do not seek out and invest in a restaurant consultant when you're having problems with cash flow, management issues, or any other of the myriad problems restaurants encounter, you're going to fight the good fight yourself. And, as you've discovered, that is very, very difficult to do. You really need somebody in your corner that has had experience combating those same problems you've either encountered or probably will encounter at some time or another. That somebody will be there to support you. You can bounce ideas off him or her and your ideas will spark other ideas, and so forth. Just as we've been doing, especially in the marketing area. As the saying goes it's lonely at the top. Why wait to discover if you're doing the right things? Instead, bring in a restaurant consultant to get another professional opinion. "Nothing lost if you know and understand the reasons for your restaurant problems, but if you don't, you just set yourself up for losses in profits and unnecessary financial worries, not to mention undue stress. Possibly even the worst case scenario: restaurant failure."

Tilly smiled. "Thankfully, I don't have that problem. Because of you, Jim, I'm beginning to feel more and more positive about recovering. Better days are ahead."

"I'm happy you think so, Tilly. I do concur. Better days are ahead. . . . Now, back to business. Customer service in your restaurant must become a priority. How you treat your customers directly affects and determines restaurant success or restaurant failure. Study what Starbucks does to ensure its guests' satisfaction. It's a revelation.

"Here's another suggestion: Word of mouth free advertising for your restaurant. Can't beat that, can you? Are you doing everything possible to take advantage of the most powerful form of free advertising? Ask yourself what you can do to get your customers spreading the good word about Aunt Tilly's Lasagna Factory. Talk up the uniqueness of your menu to customers, friends, and family. Brag a little about how good your lasagna is and invite them in for a meal. That kind of word-of-mouth advertising is golden.

"Here's another idea. How about registering for education courses in restaurant management and training? That may help you stay current with marketing trends in the food service business and understand your customers better. Every piece of additional information you learn is going to help you do a better job."

"Jim, what do you recommend as far as getting outside help . . . other than from you, of course?"

Jim grinned. "You don't need any additional help, Tilly."

They both chuckled.

Jim said, "In all seriousness, let's say you don't have the money to hire a professional restaurant consultant. The second best option is to call SCORE (Service Corps of Retired Executives), where restaurant owners and managers can tap into free professional advice from retired restaurant professionals, courtesy of the Small Business Administration."

"That's a great idea," Tilly said. "Why let all of that talent go to waste? You know, Jim, I've heard of SCORE but never used it. Can the folks there help me with marketing and promotion?"

Jim said, "They sure can, Tilly. Latch on to a retired restaurateur and my guess he or she will generate dozens of thoughts, suggestions, and ideas to help you."

"Another reason for restaurant failures is not taking a professional approach to restaurant marketing. People won't come to your restaurant just because it's there. It has to be marketed and promoted. Make a commitment right now to seek out new restaurant marketing ideas."

"Besides marketing," Tilly asked, "are there any other functions that I should keep an eye on?"

"Good question. Have someone periodically review your restaurant accounting system to see if it is well organized. In your case, ask Laura, although I'm sure you already have. She may find ways to reduce expenses, save more money, and offer ideas such as how to keep an accurate restaurant daily sales log.

"You may not know how to compare restaurant financial statements or interpret them. I suggest that you invest some time into really learning how to do this. Most local colleges teach such a course. Alternatively, you can find many such courses online.

"Along the same line, periodically check available cash against accounting records to determine how to pay daily, weekly, and monthly expenses efficiently. By that I mean not losing track of where your money is going.

"Still on the subject of accounting, not staying on top of your current liabilities vis-à-vis your current assets can damage your ability to pay your future related expenses. If your restaurant accounting system has incorrect entries, find them before they create cash flow problems and who knows what else."

"Those are all good suggestions. How about on the sales side of accounting?"

'If gross restaurant sales are lower than operating expenses, technically you're in default, and that's one short step from going out of business, so it behooves you to keep a close watch on operating expenses, including daily, weekly, and monthly follow-ups. But bear in mind those follow-ups are worthless unless and until you take corrective measures to bring operating expenses in line with gross sales. That's another area in which somebody like me can help.

"Nowadays, with the ready availability of sophisticated, yet reasonably inexpensive, costing software systems to help you manage and control the menu items, not investing in them is simply asking for higher and less controlled costs."

Tilly said, "That's one place I will definitely heed your recommendations."

"A related item, Tilly, is looking into ways to improve keeping accurate inventory of food and beverage levels. At the heart of accurate inventory records you will find both first-rate manual and computerized counting systems which tabulate inventory costs at the end of each accounting period. One of the prime reasons for restaurant failure is that inventory levels of food and beverages often are too high relative to corresponding restaurant sales levels. So make it a point to collect and review daily and weekly operating information, and take action accordingly based on what you find."

Tilly closed her notebook and pocketed her pen. "Great session, Jim. "I'm looking forward to the next."

Jim winked at Tilly. "Good news, Tilly. We're getting close to the end. You're going to graduate soon."

Chapter Sixteen

The Business Doctor Offers Tilly Tips for Controlling Costs

"Tilly, I know we've discussed costs before, but I want to emphasize them again through a series of recommendations I've made that my restaurant clients have found extremely useful."

"I'm ready when you are, Jim."

"Okay, here's the first: Examine food costs periodically, and the shorter the period the better your ability to keep food costs (or any other costs for that matter) in line with budget. One of the foundation principles of effective management is that the shorter the cycle of control, the more quickly you can respond to sub-standard performance, make corrections, get back on track, and over the longer haul stay on budget. If, for example, you catch variances to food costs weekly, you can bring them in line for the monthly report. If you wait until the end of the month, it's too late to do anything about it for that month. If you're foolish enough to check only once a quarter, you won't have many quarters before you visit the bankruptcy court."

"I've heard of that method of control. My Frank - God bless his soul - was a production manager in the Smallville furniture factory, and he told me the same thing. He used almost the same words you used, Jim."

"Frank obviously was a good manager and understood the importance of time in tracking performance, Tilly. I'm sure you miss him."

Tilly thanked Jim for the sentiment.

"Returning to the subject, The National Restaurant Association provides financial ratios for different types of restaurants and styles of service. Those numbers are available from the association. You should use those ratios to check the performance of your restaurant. When all of the components of a food management system are put in place, before long you'll be able to beat those averages."

"I remember the numbers we discussed. I have to drive down my food costs from 38 percent of gross receipts to 30 percent."

"And then set your sights on 25 percent. The difference between your present inflated food costs and your budgeted amount for food will reveal the potential cost savings, and in most cases, that number can be significant.

"It starts with purchasing. Develop a standards book, and take steps to assure that purchased products are bought and received according to specifications. Those standards should include price, quantity, quality, and delivery date. The last one, delivery date, is often overlooked, but it's important because - "

"Let me say why, Jim. It's because if the vendor ships ahead of schedule, my inventory costs will be out of line with gross receipts, and I'll take the hit in the profit and loss statement."

Jim reached over and patted Tilly's arm. "You are really and truly learning your lessons, aren't you?"

Tilly curtsied and grinned. "Under the master's guiding hand."

Jim bowed. "Thank you, madam, thank you so much. . . . To get serious again, make sure the purchased price (this does not necessarily mean the lowest price) is the best you can get for the product, and that the food quality supports the yield you expect to get."

"Recipes are the standards for yield, aren't they, Jim?"

"You're on the ball, Tilly. Also, assure that your cooks are using the right recipes, and that the cooking procedure (time, temperature, and specified equipment) in the kitchen are the same as those described in the recipe. Every now and then check yields and hold portion control to standard recipes. Ask if actual yields are the same as forecasted in the recipe, such as size, weight, looks, and taste."

"The next issue revolves around the production forecast, doesn't it?"

Jim smiled and shook his head in wonder. "Wow, what a bright pupil you are. Why don't you tell me what to look for in the production forecast?"

Tilly brought her thoughts together. "I should ask if leftover products are being utilized in the production cycle for the coming meals, are orders for product being reduced by the ingredients already in the kitchen or freezer, are the yields from a recipe being tracked, and are portion sizes accurate, are popularity ratios being used to forecast amounts to be produced and updated at least weekly by redoing the popularity index, are meals (or customer counts) being accurately tabulated every night, and if prevailing labor rates are high, and can convenience products be used to reduce labor (either purchased or made in house)? . . . How's that for a mouthful?"

Jim clapped his hands. "Tilly, you floor me. What a magnificent performance! You said that better than I ever could and, most important of all, you included all of the necessary checks to assure control of the production forecast. I'll bet you can even predict what I'm going to talk about next."

"Labor costs?"

"You get the brass ring. That's right. Labor costs."

Tilly shrugged. "Had to be. It's the remaining large cost element of restaurant operations."

Jim said, "Use typical financial ratios published by The National Restaurant Association as a guide and pursue them aggressively. Don't allow under-performing financial ratios to become a way of life, and eventually you'll reach the national averages. And, my guess is, given your determination, you'll ultimately surpass them. I've got faith in you.

Can you guess the best way to control labor costs in your restaurant?"

Tilly grinned. "I don't need to guess. Has to be scheduling. As you've explained, without proper scheduling, costs rise and customers wait for their meals. The wrong people in the right jobs spells trouble."

Jim shook his head in disbelief. "Pretty soon, you'll be taking over my job. But you're right, you need first to determine the coverage standard (number of covers or customers a wait person should be able to serve in a meal period: that's your basic standard), and use it to project the number of servers and kitchen staff needed a week in advance. Then, every night tabulate the number of meals or covers and see if there are any variances. In other words, was last week's labor hours enough to handle the number of customers and the meals served? Just as important, do the standards indicate that you have too many servers and kitchen staff? Not many restaurants can run profitably by overstaffing.

"Along that same line, Tilly, do you take into account disparities in the schedule?"

Tilly said, "Do you mean for weather, holidays, and special events when scheduling for next week's labor needs? The answer is yes. When planning the restaurant's workload for the coming week, I make allowances for such disparities."

"Let's see how good you are, Tilly. How do you plan to handle station charts?"

"That's an easy one, Jim. I've already drawn up station charts that assign tables to servers along with a list that specifies all work that can be done by servers, such as vacuuming, washing windows, and cutting garnishes." Tilly stuck out her tongue at Jim. "There!" she said.

Jim slapped his knee and roared. When he stopped laughing, he said, "You are definitely on a roll. Now tell me how you plan to handle starting and stopping times for shift work."

"I'm doing it now. I schedule wait staff with a starting time and stopping time using descriptions such as early, late, and closing, rather than specific shift times as you taught me. And, if I'm not available, I assign authority and responsibility to check the assigned side work before releasing servers for the day."

Jim started to say something but Tilly held up her hand and said, "I'm not finished. What I was about to say is that I use labor hour standards that you so graciously provided from your analytical studies of my restaurant to assign workloads to both the dining room and kitchen staffs, based on forecasted workloads."

"To make sure the number of meals planned for the week is correct?" Jim said.

"Yes, that's right. And I've started cross-training restaurant workers, so when vacations and absences occur I'm not running around like a chicken with my head cut off, trying to cover all bases. Sure makes my life easier."

"How about job descriptions?" Jim asked.

Tilly curled her finger at Jim. "Follow me."

Jim did and they went into the staging area for meals between the kitchen and dining room. Tilly pointed to the large cork bulletin board hanging on the wall. They contained posted job descriptions for all the restaurant's workers.

Jim whistled. "I see you've been burning the midnight oil."

"Time's a wasting, Jim. I've got to get back on track and do it fast."

"Anything else you think is worthwhile mentioning about labor costs, Tilly?"

Tilly gave Jim's question some thought. "Okay, here's another cost I may be able to reduce. That's the price of uniforms and linens and laundry bills for cleaning them. Technically speaking, it's not a labor cost but one closely associated with labor."

Jim nodded. "Always an important category."

Tilly continued, "These are questions I've been asking myself lately that might save money: Can I ask employees to wash and press their own uniforms? Is it possible to have linens washed at work? Should I require uniforms for the dining room staff or can black slacks and white shirts or blouses be required attire?"

"Those are legitimate questions, Tilly, and deserve looking into. . . . How about energy costs?"

"I talked with our power company representative the other day and got some really good ideas. He suggested reducing energy consumption by requiring a sequential turning on of power equipment every fifteen minutes rather than all at once at the start of the day. He says by reducing spike loads my energy bill will go down."

"A couple of final thoughts, Tilly. Ask yourself these two questions: Do you have vendors bid on chemicals for washing, and does the successful bidder train your kitchen employees in using the chemicals and associated equipment such as the dishwasher, pot and pan scrubber, and power sprayer? Finally, if interest rates have dropped, can the restaurant's mortgage be refinanced?"

~

"Okay, Tilly, that concludes the extent of my recommendations based on an analysis of your restaurant. The final point to discuss, the one I mentioned at the start of our discussions, is location."

"I think I know where this is headed, Jim, and I'm not at all sure I'm going to agree with you."

"The fact remains, Tilly, that you have ignored the three basic tenets of running a restaurant, or for that matter, any retail establishment."

"I know. Don't tell me. We've gone over this before." Tilly sighed with exasperation. "Location, location, location."

"You've got to face the ugly truth. You were in the right location in Smallville and the wrong location in Largetown. Can you accept that, Tilly?"

A silence permeated the room. Finally, Tilly said in a low voice Jim had to strain to hear, "Yes, although it kills me to admit it."

"Okay then, can you accept the fact that your business in this location is simply not drawing enough customers?"

"This is where we disagree. I want to try those marketing techniques we discussed. Surely, they'll bring in more customers."

"I'm sure they will, Tilly. But the point is how many? You're in a tight competitive race as it is, in an affluent district, with tough competitors who are more attuned to providing the kind of cuisine affluent customers demand. Your menu is more basic, the kind that appeals to regular everyday folks. Not the demographic you're in."

"You don't think the marketing techniques we discussed, Jim, will overcome that liability?"

"No, Tilly, I don't. In fact, based on my experience in similar situations over the years, I would estimate you have a five percent chance of succeeding here, and a ninety-five-percent chance of failing. I can't make it any clearer than that."

"That's really depressing. I like Largetown. I don't really want to leave."

"Think about it, Tilly, long and hard. You've got a great product but it has to find the right customers to succeed. Will you give me that much, Tilly? Will you think about it?"

Tilly glanced out the front window of the restaurant as if she could discern the answer there. "Okay," she grumbled, "I will.

Chapter Seventeen

Tilly Follows the Business Doctor's Recommendations and Succeeds Beyond Her Wildest Dreams

"Well, what do you think, Tilly?" Laura said. Both women and Bob House were touring her former restaurant in Smallville, the property she had bought, once known as Gilbert's Diner.

A ghost of a smile illuminated Tilly's face as she reminisced. "It hasn't changed much, that's for sure. It's pretty much the same." She turned to Bob. "How come they didn't replicate the typical Italian Kitchen layout?"

Laura said, "Except for this one location, you can go into any Italian Kitchen nationwide and find the exact same layout. It doesn't vary."

Bob sort of grinned. "As Italian Kitchen management told me, they were experimenting with a new concept. What they call down home country style cooking."

"How quaint," Laura said and snorted. "Nice of them to look down their long noses at us plain country folks."

Bob beckoned Tilly and Laura to follow him to the kitchen. As they walked there he said, "There was no snobbery involved, Laura. Italian Kitchen is a large corporation and this is how they test market. Believe me, if they felt there was any chance of making a buck with the concept, there would have been a thousand of these down home cooking restaurants pop up virtually overnight. What they were missing was your famous lasagna coupled with your personal charm, which customers loved."

Tilly blushed.

"I meant that sincerely," Bob said.

Tilly said "I know you did, and I do appreciate it."

She continued examining the restaurant's facilities. "It's pretty clean, very little damage done. This kitchen is spotless."

Bob said, "Italian Kitchen makes sure that all of their restaurants follow federal and state laws and local codes. And they stress maintenance and cleanliness."

Tilly said, "I can tell."

"The management said they would renovate and freshen the restaurant to your liking, Tilly. No charge."

Laura scoffed. "Pardon my cynicism, but how come they're being so generous?"

"Because," Bob said, "they have a reputation for honesty and fair play and they want to keep it that way. They don't want the town of Smallville cheated out of one of their few restaurants. That's bad publicity. Particularly after they laid an egg here. They know Tilly can make it a going concern. She's done it before."

Bob gave Tilly one of his best salesman's smiles. "Here's the best part, Tilly. The price is right." He mentioned the sales price and it was so low Tilly whistled.

"Not only that," Bob said. "They're willing to lend you the down payment at a quarter point below prime. You can't ask for any better financial package."

Laura folded her arm within Tilly's. "Well, gal, what do you say? Are you interested? Bob and I want you back here, and my guess is so do all of your former customers. If you re-open Aunt Tilly's Lasagna Factory in Smallville, I'm going to predict it will be a smashing success."

Bob nodded in agreement. "I second that. I've done some checking with local shop owners and the media. Everybody I talked with told me they miss your lasagna dishes. The paper's editor went so far as to say, confidentially of course, that his mama's lasagna didn't come close to matching yours for taste and flavor. Coming from a man that hands out compliments as often as a dog walks on its hind legs, that's high praise."

Tilly and Laura burst out laughing. Bob's face turned red. "What . . . ?" After a few moments, he joined in.

Tilly signed the contract to buy back the restaurant later that afternoon.

~

Tilly was lucky. She managed to sell her Largetown restaurant to an upscale restaurant chain that wanted a foothold in her geographical area. She used this money along with the loan she received from Italian Kitchen to buy back her former restaurant.

It was a proud day when the neon sign proudly proclaiming Aunt Tilly's Lasagna Factory was erected in front of her restaurant. Smallville's leading (and only) newspaper and the local TV station covered the event. Tilly appeared as the featured story in the newspaper, and the TV station interviewed her as she prepared the house specialty.

The publicity drew many former and new diners to Aunt Tilly's Lasagna Factory. But Tilly, now armed with an array of marketing tools she had learned from The Business Doctor, ran a special promotion every month that attracted new business. Within three months of the re-opening, Tilly was serving a full house for both lunch and dinner and planning an expansion of the restaurant. The efficient manner in which she ran her business (courtesy again of The Business Doctor) allowed her to increase her seating turnover and serve more customers.

Tilly was proud to say that she now routinely served diners from as far away as Indianapolis. Many tourists, traveling through the great state of Indiana from faraway places like New York and Los Angeles, found Aunt Tilly's Lasagna Factory and were glad they did.

Right from the opening bell, Tilly's restaurant was profitable. Within six months she paid off the loan from Italian Kitchen. What especially amazed Tilly was how relatively easy restaurant success was by simply following the procedures established for her by The Business Doctor.

Tilly also found success in her personal life. She and Bob House married and Bob became her business manager. The two of them became the talk of the town and were frequent dinner guests in the homes of Smallville's elite.

Despite Tilly's ascension to fame and fortune, there was a . . .shall we call it a maturity about her. She was no longer prone to leap wildly from Smallville to points beyond in some Hollywood fantasy of becoming the state's greatest restaurateur. Slow and steady became her motto. Under her stewardship, and aided by occasional advice from The Business Doctor, Aunt Tilly's Lasagna Factory grew both in number of meals served and profitability.

Then, a lightning strike of luck. Tilly was asked to describe her success story on the popular Rachael Ray TV show. Predictably, her appearance attracted nationwide attention. Soon after, her restaurant was reviewed by cooking experts around the country, and she became a frequent guest on radio and TV cooking shows in the Midwest.

About one month after this flurry of attention, she received a call from a representative of the frozen foods giant DownHomeDinners, Inc., the largest frozen foods company in the USA. Apparently, her success story had traveled far and wide and found its way to the desk of the chairwoman and CEO of DownHomeDinners. She was interested in buying out Aunt Tilly's Lasagna Factory and marketing Tilly's lasagna as an integral part of the DownHomeDinners frozen food family.

Shortly after that, Tilly and Bob, with Tom Cashe and Laura Booker by their sides, penned a deal that put literally millions in Tilly's pocket.

Then came that wonderful day when Tilly's frozen lasagna hit the market. She posed for the local newspaper holding one of the frozen food packages with her picture baking a lasagna dinner on the front. How proud she was; it had been a five year journey with lots of ups and downs (mostly downs) before she arrived at this point of her life.

Despite her now national fame, Tilly continued, as part of the arrangement she had with DownHomeDinners, to run Aunt Tilly's Lasagna Factory in Smallville.

Well, that's the story. Needless to say, this story has a happy ending, and so can yours, if you own or manage a restaurant. Just follow the prescriptions outlined in this book. And, if you ever travel through the great state of Indiana, stop in and say hello to Aunt Tilly and sample some of her world renowned lasagna.

She'll be happy to see you.

Appendix

101 Ways
Employees Steal
From Their
Restaurant and Bar
Employers

1. Employee doesn't ring up a sale and keeps the cash.

2. Employee under-rings the correct price of an item and pockets the difference.

3. Phantom register: An extra register in the bar for use only during specific times. For example during happy hour. The income during this period is not totaled on the master file and those funds are skimmed by clever but cheating employees.

4. Waiters/waitresses serve and collect cash from customers while the register is totaled between shift changes.

5. Waiter/waitress claims a customer walkout that never happens and keeps the money received from the customer.

6. Those with deft hands and nerves of steel swoop up the customer's cash from the table.

7. Collusion between the bartender and cocktail server resulting in fewer reported sales.

8. Phantom bottle. The bartender brings his own bottle of liquor (probably stolen from his employer) onto his shift and pockets cash from its sale.

9. Short pour. The bartender pours less than the standard shot to cover "give away" liquor costs.

10. Bartender duplicates a pour on the computerized dispenser system, resulting in dispensing and registering one shot, while short-shooting the liquor into two glasses.

11. Bartender claims a phony returned drink. This extra drink is sold by the bartender and he pockets the money.

12. Bartender gives away free drinks in anticipation of larger tips. (Only in bars with no automated cash register systems).

13. Wine steward/ bartender claims a customer broke a bottle of wine, which then appears in the breakage list. The wine steward/ bartender sells the bottle of wine or sells it by the glass, pocketing the cash.

14. Customer places money on the bar; he is served without the money being collected. The customer leaves. The bartender pockets the money without ringing up the sale.

15. Clever bartenders under-report the number of draft beers that are poured from a keg and pocket the difference.

16. Bartender under-charges for drinks with the anticipation of a larger tip.

17. Bartenders re-use register drink receipts.

18. Cocktail servers understate sales when a pre-check system is absent and walk away with a pocketful of extra money.

19. Bartender exchanges free drinks with the cook for free dinners.

20. An old one: The bartender adds water to liquor bottles to maintain inventory.

21. Another old one: The bartender sells lower priced liquor and charges for premium brands.

22. Bartender receives kickbacks from liquor distributors.

23. When the bar is selling both liquor to go (bottles) and by the drink, bartender claims missing bottles are "to go" sales.

24. One person in charge of liquor pick-up, check-in, and stocking is very tempting. That one person simply takes liquor and sells it, pocketing the money.

25. Charging regular bar prices, but ringing up at happy hour prices.

26. Servers charging for free happy hour hors d'oeuvres and bar snacks.

27. Hotel maids sell complimentary cocktail or wine coupons from a hotel room to bartenders, who exchange them for cash from the cash register.

28. Bartender claims the new register is too confusing or time consuming, and the owner lets him get away with it, because without adequate controls in place, the bartender is going to steal him blind.

29. This one is as old as the hills: Short changing customers.

30. Ringing cash sales on the service or dining room key.

31. Adding two different customer drinks together and charging both, claiming a misunderstanding in who was purchasing the round.

32. Ringing up food items on the liquor key and pocketing the difference.

33. Reselling returned beverages.

34. Free after shift drinks for the restaurant and bar staff not consumed by employees, sold to customers.

35. Providing free courtesy drinks to visiting bartenders.

36. Cooks requesting beverages for service from the kitchen and then drinking them.

37. Not pouring liquor into blended fruit drinks to cover a patron charge.

38. Draft beer system not secured at closing.
     Instead, available to janitors after hours.

39. Having the customer sign a credit card
     voucher in advance and overcharging, then
     pocketing the difference.

40. Bartender claiming that when opening the
     cash register was short, when he in truth
     he stole from the cash register.

41. Short tape. Cashier totals out the cash
     register, starts a new tape, and keeps both
     new tapes and the cash.

42. Collecting directly from customers without
     guest checks.

43. Incorrect over-ringing of checks and
     pocketing the difference.

44. Phony voiding of bar or dinner bills.

45. Selling during ribbon or tape changes and
     pocketing the cash.

46. Changing amounts on credit cards. (You
     would be surprised how often this occurs
     without customers realizing it.)

47. Running a credit card through twice.

48. Changing the guest check after the customer leaves.

49. Bartender provides service orders without ringing them up, and later rings them up for a smaller amount cash sale, pocketing the difference.

50. Placing tip jars next to the cash register. It's then easy for a customer to make a mistake and place cash for the meal in the tip jar while the bartender rings "no sale" for register activity. Guess who pockets the money in the tip jar?

51. Falsifying cumulative register readings and "losing" the cash register tape.

52. Collusion between cooks and servers.

53. Using old guest checks no longer in service.

54. Claiming a returned meal.

55. Again, an old one: Adding items that were not ordered to customers' checks.

56. Confusing customers with machine printed guest checks that are hard to read, overcharging, and pocketing the surplus.

57. Writing in food or beverages not sold to pre-check guests.

58. Improper use of the training key.

59. Phony daily reports.

60. Bookkeepers not making deposits by reporting that cash is short.

61. Bookkeepers claiming improperly written check or incorrect credit card transaction.

62. Bookkeepers writing checks to bank for FICA and pocketing the cash.

63. Bookkeepers paying fictitious bills to themselves.

64. Managers adding hours to employees' checks and splitting the difference with them.

65. Managers claiming fictitious employees on the payroll and cashing their checks.

66. One of the most abused: taking home free food or liquor or both.

67. Selling takeout orders, not writing up the bill, and pocketing the cash.

68. Employees overstating hours or changing time sheets.

69. Changing preset prices on the cash register and charging customers higher prices.

70. Over-charging on banquet sales (rampant).

71. Getting direct kickbacks from vendors.

72. Accepting lower quality meat or produce and getting cash under the table from vendors.

73. Accepting lower weights from vendors and getting kickbacks.

74. Taking home "trim" food products.

75. Cooking surplus food from the kitchen and taking the food home.

76. Making fictitious paid-outs.

77. Making fictitious coupon sales.

78. Stealing gift certificates.

79. Overusing the privilege of personal telephone calls.

80. Stealing funds from vending machines.

81. Pocketing funds from grease barrel pick-ups.

82. Keeping free samples from vendors.

83. Overstating the tip while understating the customer charge.

84. Servers ringing up coffee and going to the kitchen to exchange with cooks for free desserts.

85. Server feeding friends for free.

86. Another common one: Taking home silverware, glassware, and linen.

87. Faking a burglary and selling whatever is stolen from the restaurant.

88. Server claims child or senior prices to cashier, but charges full price and pockets the difference.

89. Server destroys guest checks and keeps the cash.

90. Employee falsifies claims that missing inventory items were returned and went bad, and sells those items to other restaurants.

91. Falsifies "sign in/sign out" time to get extra pay.

92. Employee holds back deposits meant for the bank account. This is a common ruse drug addicts use to supply their habit.

93. Employee doesn't deposit money in the bank as instructed, or deposits a lesser amount, and pockets the difference.

94. Chef purchases special food items not on the standard purchase list for employee consumption.

95. Cashier accumulates guest checks to ring up after customers leave. This enables the cashier to change amounts or delete bills and pocket the money. This is a common scam when server and cashier collude.

96. Bartender handwrites bar tabs and rings in lesser amounts into receipts.

97. Employees reuse guest checks for similar orders.

98. Kitchen staff wraps food and drops it into the garbage can for later retrieval.

99. Mobile catering drivers purchase and sell their own inventory for self-profit.

100. Chefs ask vendors to falsify invoices, and then sell food purchases to other suppliers.

101. Chefs demand gifts of a personal nature in exchange for business from vendors.

Author's Biography

Dr. James (Jim) McCain, The Business Doctor

Business Works: www.bizdrsolution.com

541 Waite Road, Rexford, NY 12148

518-383-3337

McCain97@aol.com

Jim McCain is a graduate of Eureka College and Kent State University. He spent 15 years as an Associate Professor at the State University of New York. As a senior business consultant , his experience includes work with many Fortune 500 companies, including GE, Sears and Prudential, and hundreds of consulting engagements with small and mid-size firms.

Jim is an Accredited Associate of the Institute for Independent Business and a Member of the Executive Councellor Guild.

He lives with his family in the Albany, New York area.

www.ingramcontent.com/pod-product-compliance
Lightning Source LLC
Chambersburg PA
CBHW022054210326
41519CB00054B/387